THE PROMISED LAND FOR CHILDREN

How To Improve Children's Confidence and Raise Their Self-Esteem

by

Dr. Rick Norris

with contributions from Wendy Forrest-Charde

authorHOUSE®

AuthorHouse™ UK Ltd.
500 Avebury Boulevard
Central Milton Keynes, MK9 2BE
www.authorhouse.co.uk
Phone: 08001974150

This book is a work of non-fiction. Unless otherwise noted, the author and the publisher make no explicit guarantees as to the accuracy of the information contained in this book and in some cases, names of people and places have been altered to protect their privacy.

First published by AuthorHouse 9/24/2007

ISBN: 978-1-4343-0815-3 (sc)

Printed in the United States of America
Bloomington, Indiana

This book is printed on acid-free paper.

Dr Rick Norris

Rick is a Chartered Psychologist who works in both clinical and occupational settings. He is a Visiting Consultant Psychologist at a number of NHS Trusts in the Midlands. He gained his PhD in Psychology from the University of Birmingham, where his area of expertise was Stress Management.

Rick also works as a Consultant for a range of organisations. His clients include a number of blue chip companies, such as Hewlett-Packard, Nokia, Millward Brown and Unisys. He has also worked with the AIDS charity the Terrence Higgins Trust and a number of SMEs. In addition, he is a visiting lecturer at the University of Warwick's Centre for Primary Health Care and the University of Glamorgan's Faculty of Health, Sport and Science.

Born in 1959 in Portsmouth, Rick is divorced with three children, Sam, Jack and Martha. Apart from his family, his main interests are running and keeping fit, reggae music, horse-racing and warm climates. He is also a long-suffering Pompey fan. Professionally his main interest is helping people to lead more fulfilled lives.

By the same author - The Promised Land – A Guide to Positive Thinking for Sufferers of Stress, Anxiety and Depression. Authorhouse, 2005.

Rick can be contacted through his website: www.the-promised-land.co.uk

Wendy Forrest-Charde

Wendy is an experienced classroom practitioner who works for both mainstream and special needs schools. She has recently been involved in the Emotional Literacy Project in Hampshire and works in this field on a regular basis.

During her many years of teaching, Wendy has been involved in 1:1 sessions with excluded pupils and has been fundamental in helping to change their lives. Her abilitiy to recognise and help champion the need for more Emotional Literacy in schools has led her to attend national conferences on both 'Frameworks' - how young people can become more engaged in their learning, and 'Hearts and Minds' which looks at the bigger social picture of children's needs.

She is interested in the lives and potential of Ethiopian Children and latterly has set up a Charitable organisation to give these children a 'step up' to education and Global Citizenship. This work is on-going and has been well received by the Ethiopian Partners in Education.

A Londoner born and bred, she is familiar with diversity and issues of equality. She is divorced and looks after two teenage children and a cat. Together with a passion for painting and creativity, her life long ambition is to encourage children to accept themselves for who they really are.

Further copies of this book are available online from Amazon or Waterstones bookshops.

DEDICATION AND ACKNOWLEDGEMENTS

This book is dedicated to:

Wendy's parents, Jack and Eileen Pierson, whose loving support has helped maintain her self-esteem throughout her life.

Rick's parents, Paul and Maureen Norris, who gave him the confidence and belief to find his own Promised Land.

Acknowledgements.
We would like to thank the following people who all made a contribution to helping us to complete this book.

To all the people whose experiences contributed to case studies in the book (the names and details have been changed) may you all live happy and fulfilled lives.

To Rick's children – Sam, Jack and Martha for all their encouragement and the use of their own stories.

To Glyn Morris for his enthusiastic and wise editorial comment.

To Sue Wolton who graciously agreed to proof read the manuscripts and offer some helpful suggestions.

To Rosemary Williams who also read the manuscript and kindly assisted with many of the corrections.

To Rosie Riley for painstakingly critiquing the book and generously sharing her marketing expertise.

TABLE OF CONTENTS

INTRODUCTION.

Rick's first book, 'The Promised Land – a guide to positive thinking for sufferers of stress, anxiety and depression' (1) proved to be very successful in helping people to change their thinking patterns in order to combat the problems of psychological distress.

The models used by Rick in 'The Promised Land' seem to make sense to most people. The way in which he explains the workings of our minds when we succumb to stress, anxiety and depression appear very straightforward. 'The Promised Land' provides many useful stories and case studies that make it easy and interesting to read for anyone who doesn't have much knowledge of psychology or medicine. In short, Rick thought he'd written a book that could benefit anyone who was suffering from psychological distress – but he was wrong.

It was only when Wendy contacted Rick that he realised he'd missed out a huge chunk of the population, namely, children aged between 5 and 16. Wendy has worked with children for 25 years and her experience suggested that children are just as likely to suffer from psychological distress as adults. Recent research from The Mental Health Foundation (2) supports this view, it estimates that 20% of children and adolescents are experiencing psychological problems at any one time.

So, with Wendy's help, Rick set out to try to produce a book aimed at helping parents, grandparents, childminders and teachers to build children's self-confidence. 'The Promised Land for Children' is our best effort. It isn't perfect, but it will work if the models, ideas and exercises are used regularly and consistently. Improving children's confidence is not a particularly difficult task if you follow the recipe in this book – but that doesn't mean it isn't hard work. Rick's ideas have helped literally thousands of adults change their thinking patterns to allow them to become more positive about themselves and their lives. Wendy's expertise has been utilised to make these ideas more applicable to a younger audience.

Training the mind is like training the body. In order to become fit we need to exercise regularly. It is not enough to take up jogging for 10 weeks and then declare we are fit for life. For many fit people exercise is a habit they never lose. To develop a healthy level of self-confidence takes the same application. One of the greatest gifts we can give our children is self-esteem. To do this we have to provide our children with the tools to develop their confidence, and the encouragement to make a habit of using these tools regularly throughout their lives.

How to use this book.

The book is divided into two parts. Part I provides an understanding of how children become stressed, anxious or depressed. Part II provides a programme of exercises to help children change their way of thinking. Many people want to rush on to Part II because this includes the practical exercises that will help their children. However, it's really important to read Part I first because it will help you understand how the mind of a child experiencing stress, anxiety and depression works – you won't be as effective in helping your children if you don't have this knowledge.

Make use of the summaries at the end of each chapter. Some readers prefer to skim through the summaries *before* they read each chapter as this helps to 'signpost' the main points. There are blank pages for your notes at the end of the book after the appendices. Some people prefer to make notes on each page whilst they are reading the book which can be very helpful as it assists in retaining the information. Be bold, don't be afraid of writing in the book, it's designed as a practical tool not an academic reference book.

The appendices at the end of the book can be photocopied and used by children to help them complete various exercises. If you have any helpful suggestions, tips or feedback please share them with us at: www.the-promised-land.co.uk

Thank you.

Part I

*How children become stressed,
anxious and depressed.*

CHAPTER 1
A STATISTICAL REMINDER OF A
WORLD THAT DOESN'T CARE.

Before we embark on the journey of how to improve our children's self-confidence and esteem it helps if we look at the context of the world in which they live, and how its changed in the last 50 years. Self-esteem and self-confidence grow out of an appreciation of who we are - the more stable and happy our upbringing, the greater the likelihood that we will feel positive about who we are as people. The less stability and support we have as children then the more likely we are to be prone to psychological distress later in life.

In this chapter we'll look at some of the changes that have occurred within society over the last 50 years and we'll trace the links between these changes and the increasing levels of psychological ill health.

Family Life.
In the 1950s family life was very different to the way that we live in the 21st century. The societal norm was for most children to come from a reasonably stable family background, with mum, dad and siblings all living under one roof. They may also have had members of the extended family, such as grandparents or aunts, uncles, and cousins living close by. The family unit appeared, at least on the face of it, to be much more closely bonded. Often, ageing grandparents would live in the same house as their children and grandchildren. Children had the opportunity to develop relationships with, not just both their parents, but with their siblings and their extended family. In most respects this was a very healthy state of affairs, indeed, it's something that is maintained in many cultures outside the UK and for some of the ethnic minority cultures within this country.

In the 21st century the family unit for many people has changed radically compared to the 1950s model. For example, relationships seem to break down with far greater frequency than they used to.

Separation and divorces are more commonplace now than they've ever been. In the UK in 1961 there were just over 27,000 divorces. In 2003 there were over 166,000 (1). The institution of marriage is also generally in decline: in England and Wales in 2001 there were only 249,227 marriages. This is the lowest annual number of marriages since 1897 and continues the long-term downward trend that began in 1973. In terms of the relative stability of family life this suggests that the comparative picture between the 1950s and the 21st century reveals a much less stable family environment in recent years.

The birth rate has also dropped dramatically in the last 40 years. It was a commonly held belief in Britain for many years that we were a nation who produced an average of '2.4 kids'. However, birth rates are falling in the UK. Over the last few years the Total Fertility Rate (number of children born per woman) has decreased from the baby boom high of 2.95 in 1964 to 1.71 in 2003 (2). This would suggest that many children today are born into families where they don't have the support of siblings with whom they can share the worries and fears they may experience in childhood.

The net effect of all these changes means that our children may not have the same levels of emotional support as previous generations.

The world of work.
In the 1950s most people simply worked to live, and it was fairly typical for people to maintain their jobs over a lifetime. There were fewer career choices and people worked to ensure that they had sufficient money to meet their basic needs. Fifty years ago it wasn't uncommon for someone to spend their entire career with one employer. In the 21st century it's very different. John Schwartz (3), in a recent article on workplace stress in the New York Times, quoted the research of Richard Sennett, a sociologist at New York University, who calculated that the average American with two years of college education will change jobs eleven times before retirement. Sennett suggests that most of the job changes occur because people are dissatisfied with their work. In modern times work seems to have

assumed a much greater level of importance in people's lives than it used to occupy, with a consequent potential cost to family life.

After both the First and Second World Wars there was an assumption that women would move more firmly into the world of work. Many women had worked in munitions factories and on farms in order to arm and feed the nation whilst the male population were away fighting. However, whilst it was true that the Second World War, in particular, changed attitudes to women in the work place, the changes were somewhat cosmetic. After the Second World War it became more common to see women in work, but they worked in certain types of roles such as administrative and support jobs – secretarial work, nursing and primary school teaching roles would have been fairly typical jobs for women in the 1950s and 1960s (4). Often the income earned by women was much less than the equivalent salary earned by men and it was seen as 'pin money', which was nice to have, but not essential to maintain a decent lifestyle.

More recently, however, there has been a dramatic rise in women's employment. In 1971 45% of households with dependent children were dual earners compared with 66% in 1999. (5). In 2005 it is estimated that 70% of women of working age were in employment (6) which again contrasts sharply with the world of the 1950s.

Another assumption in the 1950s was that women would leave work once they became pregnant and would not return to the world of work until their children were themselves adults, if they returned at all. In 2005 53% of women with children were in employment (7) and 63% of women who worked before having a child returned to work within 12 weeks of having the baby and over half of these mothers returned to full time work.

The concept of working mothers is a fairly recent phenomenon as the statistics suggest. Many women in the workplace are balancing work and looking after a family, often they are also single parents. However, it's not simply the case that women need to earn an income to support their families. The number of women in the world of work has increased because many women are now making a positive choice to return to, or continue in, their careers.

Whilst, in many respects, the number of women in the work place is a positive thing, it has had an effect on 'traditional' family life. This, in turn, seems to have implications for the incidences of psychological distress as we seek to get the balance between work and life.

The elusive work/life balance.
In the 1950s work was seen as a means to an end. The end was survival: people went to work because it provided them with the means to live. Arguably, this simplistic model resulted in many families in the 1950s having a clear work life balance. Today, the picture is very different. People are concerned about the intrinsic nature of the work itself and what meaning or value this adds to their existence. Paradoxically, however, family, leisure, travel and our physical and spiritual well being are increasingly viewed as more important than work for many people. People want to take advantage of all the opportunities that exist in life. Our expectations of life have been raised and therefore it's not surprising that our expectations of work have also been increased. This paradox makes it difficult to get a balance between work and life and potentially it is our children who could lose out.

In the 21st century it has also become much more difficult to know where the boundaries are between work and life. Mobile phones mean we are far more accessible than we used to be so it's easy for work colleagues to call us about a problem regardless of where we are. Lap top computers with fast connections to the Internet mean we can take work with us whenever and wherever we want. Rick works with an Irish executive from Dublin called Sean who takes his mobile phone and laptop computer with him on holiday. He works from the side of the hotel swimming pool where he conducts conference-calls with the rest of his management team spread throughout both Eire and Northern Ireland, whilst adjusting the figures on the spreadsheet of his lap top computer.

It would be easy to put the sole blame for the difficulty in achieving a work/life balance on employers' expectations of their employees, however, the real picture is more complicated. Research by Deeks (8) shows that we don't necessarily view work as an intrusion into our home lives. His study suggested that 70% of people in a pan European survey were interested in tele-working from home. This seems to reflect a much more complex relationship with a world of work where technology is identified as both a negative and a positive influence. This highlights just how elusive the balance between work and life can be. The contrast between the 21st Century search for work/life balance and the reality of the 1950s model of work/life balance is quite stark, and it's our children who potentially suffer the brunt of the modern imbalance.

Psychological Distress.
Over the last 50 years there has been a huge increase in the prevalence of psychological disorders and some of this increase is due, at least in part, to the factors listed above. Despite the facts that modern workplaces are safer than ever and we are, in relative terms, far better off than our parents or grandparents, we continue to experience worrying trends in sickness absence from work.

In 2004, work place absences rose for the first time in five years. It's particularly interesting to note the proportion of days lost due to psychological distress. An increasing number of days are lost through various forms of psychological distress each year. Stress was cited as the second biggest cause of sickness absence for non-manual workers in the UK for the year 2002-2003 (9). Many of these cases end up in long term sickness, which accounts for around 13 million days' absence per year and costs the UK £3.8 billion (10). The World Health Organisation reported that in 2001 there were 340 million people suffering from depression (11).

In 'The Promised Land', Rick suggested that a lot of this psychological illness is due to the fact that our expectations of life have increased greatly. The expectation is driven from our own views; the views of our family, friends and work colleagues; and also by the messages put out by an increasingly powerful media which influences so many aspects of our lives. We feel the pressure to have a successful career, well-adjusted children, a perfect relationship with our partner, the ideal home, the latest technology – in short we feel we need to have it all and to have it now. The consequence of this 21st century phenomenon is the increasing level of adult stress, anxiety and depression, which also affects the psychological well being of the children of those adults.

Recent research suggests that despite our increasing affluence in material terms we are less happy than we've ever been. The World Health Organisation (12) suggests that depression is much less common in undeveloped nations where people are much less affluent than the populations of most western countries. The same report estimates that 15% of the population in developed countries will suffer from depression at some point in their lives. In June 2006 BBC TV made a series of programmes entitled the 'The Happiness Formula'. In the programme, researchers from the London School of Economics posed the question "What is the recipe for happiness?" One of their key conclusions was that friendship had a much bigger impact on happiness than income.

In summary, the world of the 21st century is very different to that of the 1950s. Family life has changed radically for many children growing up today as a result of a variety of socio-economic factors. The relationship we have with our work is also significantly more complex than the relationship that our grandparents experienced with their work. Many people's expectations of both work itself and life in general have increased hugely, with much of this expectation being unrealistic. Consequently, the increase in our unrealistic expectations is a major contributor to the elevated levels of psychological distress experienced in modern day life, a phenomenon which is now beginning to manifest itself in the nation's children, as well as the adult population.

Summary of Chapter 1
A statistical reminder of a world that doesn't care.

Family Life.
The contrast between family life in the 1950s and the 21st century is quite stark and the consequent effect on children in terms of reduced emotional support is significant. The family unit has changed quite radically with a number of factors contributing to this. The number of marriages is falling and the number of divorces is increasing which means that fewer children are brought up in homes where both parents are present. Falling birth rates have meant that children grow up in smaller families with fewer siblings. Whilst it was not uncommon for families in the 1950s to have three, or even four, generations under one roof, this is far less common today. The net effect of these changes means that children have fewer sources of emotional support than in previous generations.

The world of work.
The world of work also reflects some significant societal changes. One factor is the greater number of women entering the workplace and staying there for longer than their mothers or grandmothers. This means many women have well established careers, which they want to return to after they have had children, An increasing number of women also opt to return to work full time, rather than part time, after the birth of a child. Another factor is the changing relationship we have with our employers. We now have far higher expectations of work than our grandparents had. It is no longer enough for work to provide the means to feed our bodies, it also has to nurture our existence. However, much of our expectation of work, or even life, may be somewhat unrealistic and this can fuel our sense of dissatisfaction.

The elusive work/life balance.
The consequence of these factors means that getting a balance between our work and our lives outside work has become increasingly difficult in the 21st century. In part this is due to employers' increased

requirements of their employees and advances in technology, such as lap top computers, mobile phones and instant access to the Internet. It is also partly driven by employees' desire to spend some time working from home in situations where the technology and the role allow.

Psychological Distress.
Despite the advances of technology and the greater affluence of the 21st century we are suffering from greater levels of psychological distress than ever before. The pressures of modern society are relentless, and our children's confidence and self-esteem may be suffering as a result.

CHAPTER 2
TIME TOUGH.

In the previous chapter, we looked at how the 21st century differs from the world of the 1950s. The result of these changes is that there is an increasing amount of data suggesting that the population in general, including children, are experiencing higher levels of psychological distress than ever before. PAPYRUS (1) a voluntary organisation committed to the prevention of young suicide, through research and support groups, has made the following observations from their research:

- In the UK, suicide is now the second most common cause of death (after road accidents) in the 15-24 age group.
- Each year approximately 500 males and 100 females in this age group take their own lives. It should be noted that whilst women make more attempts on their lives than men, their choice of less violent methods, for example drug overdose, means their survival rates are far higher than those of men, who typically select more violent methods such as hanging or shooting (2).
- Half of those who commit suicide are not classified as mentally ill.

In order for us to help improve children's self-confidence we need to understand a little bit more about psychological distress in general and depression in particular.

Psychological distress and depression.
Psychological distress comes in many forms and can be described by a whole range of negative emotions, such as anger, anxiety, fear, sadness, stress or frustration. We experience psychological distress as part of our everyday lives and more often than not we are able to cope with 'feeling a bit down'. However, psychological distress is potentially damaging to us and if it persists, unchecked, for any

length of time it can lead to depression, which is significantly more debilitating than just 'feeling a bit down'. Ultimately, psychological distress can also affect our physiology. Research in Japan (3) suggests that a hugely disproportionate percentage of heart attacks are suffered on a Monday morning when people are preparing to start their working week. The stress experienced by some people at the thought of beginning another working week can lead to significant surges in blood pressure, which can cause heart attacks.

Perhaps the most widely known form of psychological distress is depression. It is often said that depression is caused by a chemical imbalance in the brain. In many cases there is a reduction in the amount of certain neurotransmitters – monoamines such as serotonin and norepinephrine. However, regarding depression as just a chemical imbalance wildly misconstrues the disorder (4). The drop in norepinephrine and serotonin levels in the brain seems to be a result of over-arousal from negative introspective thinking patterns and a lack of participation in activities that we enjoy doing.

It has become increasingly common for doctors to be asked to prescribe anti-depressants for children to combat the chemical imbalance in the neurotransmitters described above. However, not only are these drugs quite powerful, they have potentially worrying side effects and can be quite addictive. Whilst medication has its place in the treatment of depression, it's important to remember that drugs don't address the causes of depression, they only address the symptoms. Many of the drugs are only licensed for short term use and are not suitable for a 'lifetime' of depression. Although drugs can be effective in treating the symptoms of the chemical imbalance, they don't affect the cause of depression - negative introspective thought patterns and a lack of participation in pleasure giving activities.

Depression, in simple terms, occurs when our heads become full of negative thoughts about our lives and ourselves. Consequently, we just can't face the effort of doing anything to cheer ourselves up, and children can be just as prone to this as adults.

The imbalance in chemicals is clearly implicated in depression, but both neurophysiological and psychological causes are implicated in depression. The US National Institute of Mental Health (5) found that the influence of genes plays an important role in vulnerability, and early life deprivation can lead to changes in brain function that increase susceptibility to depressive symptoms. Later in the book we will look at the effects of nature and nurture and children's susceptibility to psychological distress in more detail.

Many people don't seem to be able to comprehend that children can suffer from stress, anxiety and depression. Those who have never suffered from depression may not understand how debilitating it is when our neurotransmitters cause the chemical imbalance in our brains. People who don't understand the problems of psychological distress are often not particularly sympathetic to sufferers. In part, this lack of sympathy is based on the idea that it's 'all in your mind' and people just need to 'pull themselves together'. Psychological distress is not as obvious as a physical injury, such as a broken leg, consequently mental health problems can be perceived as somehow less real. It may appear that having a head full of negative thoughts is a straightforward problem to put right. However, such is the power of the unconscious mind that once we become locked into this pattern of negative thinking it can suck us dry of any positive emotions and ultimately, in a number of tragic cases, it robs some adults and children of the will to live.

One of the clearest examples of children having suicidal thoughts is the case of Graham, a young man who Rick worked with. Graham's parents and brother regularly physically abused Graham from an early age. During counselling Graham recalled that he had planned his first suicide at the age of seven. He planned to eat his pencils in the hope of causing himself lead poisoning. Graham was very disappointed to learn, soon after making his plan, that modern pencils were made from graphite, which is not poisonous. Suicide became part of a very natural thinking pattern for Graham throughout his childhood and early adult years. In a paradoxical sense the suicide plans played a part in keeping Graham alive until he was finally able to defeat his negative thinking patterns in his early 30s.

In 2005 the Centre for Suicide Research (6) carried out a school based study using an anonymous questionnaire to look at the true prevalence of deliberate self-harm (DSH) in 6,020 young people, aged 15 -16. The statistics revealed that 13.2% of the sample studied had engaged in DSH, with self-cutting as the commonest method used by about half of those children who self-harmed and in almost equal proportions between boys and girls.

Over the years, Wendy has worked with a wide range of children who have suffered from stress, anxiety and depression. All these children have experienced difficult problems in their lives. A good example was Justin, a thirteen-year-old boy who became dependent on cannabis following the separation of his parents during a volatile divorce. When his mother began a relationship with the man who later became his stepfather, Justin started to trash his bedroom, self-harm and steal from shops before he was eventually referred for psychological support.

Another case was that of Shakira, a fourteen-year-old girl, who was so badly bullied that she could not face going to school. Shakira became literally rigid with fear and could not leave the house until she was eventually referred to a unit for depressed and anxious young women.

One child Wendy dealt with, Liam, was only eight when his mother abandoned him and left the family home for Cyprus, taking Liam's younger brother with her.

This small selection of cases shows the variety of difficult situations that many children face early on in their lives. The distress experienced in these situations can lead to a whole raft of both psychological and physiological problems. Psychological symptoms include: the inability to concentrate on any task for very long; seemingly irrational fears; being unable to complete even simple tasks without making errors; experiencing disproportionately strong negative emotions, such as anger or sadness, in response to seemingly minor incidents; feeling suicidal; or even a numbness to any feeling at all. The physiological symptoms are just as varied: sleeplessness; loss of appetite; skin disorders; depletion of the immune system leading to increased susceptibility to infections; high blood pressure; and in adults even heart disease and cancer are implicated in the aetiology of psychological distress.

So, whilst stress, anxiety and depression may not appear to be complex issues, the effects can be very harmful and if unchecked they are potentially fatal. In the next part of this chapter we'll try to explain how we can go from having negative introspective thoughts about our lives to the possibility of developing life threatening physiological and psychological symptoms.

The mind as a DVD library.
Rick first used this explanation in his book 'The Promised Land' (7) and most people find it's a pretty 'sticky' idea - Rick likens the working of the mind to a library full of DVDs - an explanation that the vast majority of adults and children understand very easily.

Imagine you have a library full of DVDs in your head. For every day of your life there is a DVD memory recorded and stored in your mind's library. Most psychologists believe in the theory of permanent memory. In other words, everything we experience is stored away in our minds. However, our recall system isn't very good and we struggle to recall memories at will, but we often find that certain sights, sounds, smells or tastes can trigger a particular memory.

For example, Rick was driving along in the car recently with his three children and the song 'Shy Guy' came on the radio. The children immediately started to recall a summer holiday they had spent in Portsmouth a few years earlier. The song 'Shy Guy' had triggered the memory of the holiday because whilst they were in Portsmouth that week Rick had bought a CD by the band Aswad which included a version of 'Shy Guy'. During the week's holiday Rick had played the album constantly. Consequently, several years later, the song 'Shy Guy' still had the power to start the DVD holiday memories playing in the minds of his children.

So, we have a huge catalogue of DVD memories stored in our mind's library. In simple terms, some of the DVDs appear to be very positive memories, some appear very negative and many seem to be neutral. When children are faced with personal challenges that are difficult to cope with they tend to play recent DVD memories that are predominantly negative. If the personal challenges persist for any length of time, children can find it increasingly difficult to play either positive DVD memories or to see any positive aspects of predominantly negative DVD memories.

If, for example, a teenage child is experiencing problems at home they may turn to drugs or alcohol in an effort to blot out the painful, negative memories. Wendy has come across many cases of teenagers who have been caught bringing drugs or alcohol into school with the consequence that they have been excluded from school. Although the exclusion is, at first, short term, there is usually a Governors meeting in the interim to discuss whether the child should be allowed back into school. This can take weeks and during this time the child often begins to play many negative DVDs about their situation. The negativity can turn into anger at the school and then anger at themselves. The anger frequently manifests itself through the child engaging in violence towards property, other people or themselves. The case of Justin we cited earlier is a good example of this.

The negative DVD memories are evoked by the focus on the psychological distress the child is currently experiencing. Eventually, these DVD memories become invasive thoughts that appear in the mind of the sufferer all the time and it becomes very hard for the child to stop these DVD memories from spinning around. Many people who haven't suffered from the effects of psychological distress don't understand how difficult it is to 'switch off' the DVD player.

It's more straightforward to change our thought patterns when we are conscious of the links between the triggers and the memories. So, if a particular song is linked to a sad time in our lives it makes sense to choose not to play that song. However many of the triggers are less obvious and are sometimes difficult to avoid.

Shakira, who we mentioned earlier, would find that simply the sight of anyone wearing the uniform of her school was enough to evoke painful memories of being bullied. Not only did Shakira experience very strong psychological reactions to this trigger but she would also go literally rigid with fear.

Children suffering from psychological distress may be unaware that a sub-conscious trigger has caused the negative DVD to start playing. The following example explains how subtle some of the triggers can be. Emma, a young woman Rick worked with, experienced severe bullying at school because of her weight.

Emma later became a sales representative travelling around the country visiting customers. After a few months at her new job she noticed that she often found herself playing the negative, painful DVDs of being bullied when she visited a particular customer who she called on regularly twice a month. During the course of her therapy Rick tried to help her recall exactly what might have triggered the DVDs. Eventually, Emma recalled that she passed a sign on a stretch of dual carriageway a few miles from the customer's factory. The sign read 'Millet's Farm Store'. Emma was not remotely interested in farm stores and had never consciously noticed the sign. The sign had appeared in Emma's peripheral vision as she was concentrating on her driving, but until her therapy the DVD memory of the sign remained in Emma's sub-conscious mind.

The sign had triggered the DVDs of the bullying because the main perpetrator of the bullying was a girl named Mandy. The link between Mandy and the sign was quite subtle. When Emma was younger she had read the 'Milly, Molly, Mandy' books by Joyce Lankester-Brisley. The name of the farm store, 'Millet' was quite close to the name 'Milly' and this sub-consciously brought the name 'Mandy' into Emma's mind. In turn, this had caused the negative DVDs of the bullying to start playing. The relevance of this story is that it demonstrates how hard it can be to prevent negative DVDs from coming into our minds because of the subtle sub-conscious nature of some triggers.

The idea that we may have the ability to press the stop button for the DVD memory and eject it from our minds is a difficult concept to accept for many children who suffer from psychological distress. However, it is the continual playing of the invasive negative DVD memories that starts to affect the levels of the neurotransmitters in the brain and once this occurs, the depressive cycle is underway. As we will see later, this can lead to negative 'memories' being created about the possible future outcome of an event. So when we use the word 'memory' in this book it can relate to both past events and future possible outcomes. Once the seed has been sown in a child's mind that a future outcome could go horribly wrong there is a danger that the child will then experience negative self-fulfilling prophecy.

In Part II of the book we'll explain several exercises to help children to create positive DVDs of how they would like the future to look. This can assist children in understanding how they can then create positive self-fulfilling prophecies.

The curse of self-doubt.
If children continually play negative DVD memories it begins to lead to self-doubt and the belief that they are to blame for what has happened to them. They then start to feel that they are inadequate to deal with their situation, that they should have done something different or even that they should have been somebody different. With almost all the 'problem' children Wendy has worked with over many years, self-doubt features very highly. One six-year-old child, Harry, had never written anything at school except his name. Harry was so frightened of failure that he felt it was better to write nothing rather than risk failure. Wendy eventually persuaded Harry to write by getting him to use a puppet to hold the pencil and then write a few words.

Kelly, in contrast, was excellent at writing. However, she seemed to have less ability for maths. She was constantly reminded, by her parents, that she wasn't good at sums and this sowed the seed of self-doubt to the point where any confidence she may have had in her maths ability dissipated completely.

Self-doubt leads to a lack of confidence, so offering a child suffering from stress, anxiety or depression the advice to "pull yourself together" is at best unhelpful and at worst it simply reinforces the self-doubt they are already experiencing.

The greater the self-doubt, the more depressed the child's mood may become. The more depressed they are then the less inclined they feel to take part in activities that previously gave them any pleasure. The less they take part in any enjoyable activities then the more likely that recent memories will be labelled as negative DVDs and stored as such in the library. And so the cycle continues.

The reticular activating system – the brain's filter.
Even if a psychologically distressed child experiences a positive or happy event during their day this is often filtered out. So when the DVD memory for the day is recalled at night it is perceived as another depressing episode in the life of the child. Ultimately this leads the child to experience increasingly low levels of self-esteem.

Our mind is a very complex piece of equipment. Psychologists admit that we still don't understand exactly how it works. What does seem clear is that our mind operates at both a conscious and sub-conscious level and between the two there is a cluster of brain cells, which acts as a filter - the reticular activating system (RAS). The filter allows certain information to go from the sub-conscious mind to the conscious mind depending on its relevance.

Wendy's experience in Reception classes with quite young children offer some wonderful insights into how much information gets filtered out and what information is deemed relevant by different children. Wendy might, for example, have organised a visit from a clown or from the Guide Dogs Association in the morning, and at the end of the day Wendy would ask the children what they remembered about their day. Often the children would mention something that happened in the last hour because it was the most recent memory. Alternatively, a hungry child may say that lunch was the best thing about the day. Or a child may focus on a tiny, yet relevant, element of the day, for example "I lost my ball."

To explain this to children give them the following exercise. Ask them to make a mental note of how many red cars they see on the journey home from school. The next time you see them ask them to tell you how many silver cars they noticed on the journey home. You'll probably get a very blank look and a confused explanation of how they had not been aware of any silver cars because you told them to focus on red cars. However, they'll usually concede that there must have been silver cars present on their journey home because in the UK it's the most common colour of car. The silver cars didn't register on their conscious mind because the filter was only allowing red cars into their conscious mind. They *saw* the silver cars, but the silver cars just didn't make it through the filter from the sub-conscious to the conscious mind. It's the same when we are experiencing some kind of psychological distress; the filter allows things that are related to our distress into the conscious mind because they seem more significant.

If the filter is set to allow the negative DVD memories of a child's life into their conscious mind then inevitably these increase the child's levels of self-doubt. If the filter only allows through DVDs showing past difficulties and the potential threats and dangers in a situation, then self-doubt begins to creep into their mind and destroys their self-confidence. The diagram below helps to illustrate this.

The DVD Library and the filter.

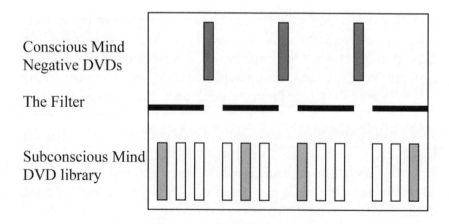

20

Matt was 13 years old. His mum, Karen, and his dad, Kevin, had been divorced for a few years. Karen did a wonderful job of trying to bring up Matt and his stepsister Charlotte. Unfortunately, Kevin who was supposed to visit Matt regularly was very unreliable. He was often late to pick Matt up and sometimes he didn't turn up at all. Matt would be visibly hurt at what he perceived to be his dad's rejection of him. On one occasion, Kevin had promised that he would take Matt camping. When Kevin turned up, late again, he told Matt that he couldn't afford to take him camping because he had to go to work to earn extra money to pay for repairs to his car.

Camping became a highly significant symbol to Matt – a symbol that made him question whether his dad loved him. A couple of days later Matt mentioned to his mum that it seemed like all his mates were going camping that summer. Of course it wasn't *all* his mates but it just seemed like that to Matt because every time anyone mentioned camping it filtered into Matt's conscious mind because of the emotional significance he now attached to camping.

Children experiencing psychological distress have their filters set to notice the negative things in their lives and consequently that's what they see and hear. Of course the negative things are there, but so are positive things. It's simply that the good things remain in the background of the sub-conscious mind - they just don't have the same level of significance. The more that the child filters out the positive DVD memories and filters in the negative DVD memories then the greater their level of self-doubt.

Summary of Chapter 2
Time tough.

Psychological distress and depression.
Psychological distress has many forms – anxiety, fear, anger, guilt, stress and perhaps the most common form, depression. Depression results from the combination of a focus on negative introspective thoughts and a lack of participation in pleasure giving activities. The negative thoughts can emanate from a whole variety of different problems children may face in their lives. Over a period of time, if a child continually has negative thoughts, it can cause a decrease in the levels of the neurotransmitters norepinephrine and serotonin in the brain. These neurotransmitters are associated with feelings of well being.

The mind as a DVD library.
When children are psychologically distressed they sub-consciously start to do two things. Firstly, they play the predominantly negative DVD memories from the past. Secondly, they find it increasingly difficult to focus on the positive aspects of any of their DVD memories.

The curse of self-doubt.
A child's negative DVD memories contain images of them in situations where they are struggling to cope and this causes them to doubt their ability to handle the situation successfully. In turn this starts to negatively impact on their self-esteem.

The reticular activating system – the brain's filter.
The reason that children in these situations find themselves focussing on negative DVD memories is because the RAS filter draws their conscious mind to anything linked to the psychological distress they are suffering. The filter allows negative DVDs from their subconscious into their conscious mind. The filter makes sure the positive DVDs are left in the child's subconscious mind and these go relatively unnoticed.

CHAPTER 3
I NEVER THOUGHT IT WOULD HAPPEN.

In the previous chapter we talked about the mind as a DVD library and how continually playing negative DVDs increases the likelihood of self-doubt in the mind of a child. In this chapter we will look at the links between playing negative DVDs and becoming a pessimist. Pessimists are less likely to believe that future outcomes will be positive, whereas optimists are more likely to believe future outcomes will be positive. Viewing negative DVDs about past events fuels pessimism because negative DVD memories of the past project the idea that future events may also be negative. Research by Kensinger and Schacter (1) suggests that in some ways we may all have a tendency towards pessimistic thinking. The study found that our memory of negative events seems to be much more accurate than for positive events. However, whilst this may be true for all of us, it doesn't explain why some people are more pessimistic than others.

Self-doubt, threat sensitivity, risk aversion and pessimism.
In the previous chapter we cited research which suggested that genetic influence and early life experiences play an important role in our tendency towards depression. Early life deprivation can lead to changes in brain function that increase susceptibility to depressive symptoms. Simply put, some children, through no fault of their own, are more prone to self-doubt than others. This predisposition to self-doubt that some children have, manifests itself through 'threat sensitivity'. Some children are very aware of the possible dangers in life: they are quite literally more sensitive than their peers to potential threats in almost any situation. As a result of this ability to sense threat they become very cautious about life and consequently are much less likely to take risks, hence the term 'risk averse'. Children who are prone to threat sensitivity and risk aversion can always see where something might go wrong – they are nature's pessimists.

It helps if we know why certain individuals find the thought of taking risks very stressful. Rick's work in clinical settings has helped to identify three factors, which, if they are present early in a child's life account for the negative thinking patterns associated with threat sensitivity, risk aversion and pessimism.

The first factor is that the threat sensitivity emanates from either the effects of nature or nurture (or both). Threat sensitive parents can easily influence some children. These parents view the world as a dangerous place and reinforce this view in their offspring. Such parents can often be heard repeatedly telling their children to be careful, or warning them of the dangers of doing certain things. A good example of this was Sajeed, a child with whom Wendy worked. He constantly re-arranged his school equipment in a neat order on his desk, with everything precisely set in its place. This rearranging behaviour occurred frequently throughout the day. The main reason that Sajeed was almost obsessive about his equipment was due to his heightened concern that other children might steal it if he didn't pay it constant attention. Sajeed's mother constantly reinforced this negative message to Sajeed.

A second factor, which can happen to people either as children or young adults, is where something very traumatic happens to them, often in the form of some type of serious mental, physical or sexual abuse. Sadly, this is something that Rick comes across all too frequently with the adults he counsels. Graham, whom we mentioned earlier in the book, was a particularly poignant example of this. He had spent much of his childhood years being ritually beaten jointly by his mother and brother when he was quite young and later by his father when he became a teenager. Under such circumstances it was no surprise to find that Graham became quite threat sensitive.

The third factor is where a child or young person is brought up in circumstances whereby they experienced generalised anxiety over a period of time. Examples of this may include: parents divorcing; moving house and changing schools on one or more occasions; long term illness; or difficult financial circumstances. Scott was a good example of this. He grew up as an only child with ageing parents.

His father was ill for many years and he frequently worried about what would happen to himself and his mother financially if his father died.

The dangers of pessimism.

It seems that some children, like those in the previous examples, are more prone to pessimism than others because they had their filters primed to notice the negative DVDs early in their lives. The negative effects of pessimism have been well documented in recent years. The writers Donald Clifton and Tom Rath (2) have produced some excellent work linking pessimism to lower life expectancy, poor health and less success in life generally. Martin Seligman, in his research on optimism and pessimism, notes that at work, school and in sport, optimists stay with difficult and challenging situations whilst pessimists don't do so well and often give up. Seligman and Schulman's (3) classic experiment showed this quite clearly. They studied life insurance sales people, an industry where sales people experience frequent rejection and have a high drop out rate. Seligman and Schulman found that the sales people who were the most optimistic significantly out performed those who were pessimistic.

Of course, not every child who was brought up in an environment of anxiety or fear goes on to be threat sensitive. Not all children who had parents who were themselves prone to worrying turn out to be pessimistic. Not every child who experiences a trauma when they are relatively young goes on to be susceptible to depression in later years. However, children who are unfortunate enough to have had their filter set to notice the negative DVD memories in life when they were relatively young will be more **likely** to have a predisposition towards suffering stress, anxiety and depression.

Some children have a predisposition to thinking in a pessimistic fashion because of the effects of one or more of these three factors early on in their lives. However, all children are capable of becoming pessimistic when they experience difficult life events, as we shall see later on in the book. Pessimism, as we noted earlier, is brought about when a child continually plays negative DVDs about past and present events. This then starts to sow the seed of doubt that leads them to believe they will be unable to cope successfully with future events. This, in turn, creates behaviours that actually make a successful outcome less likely – negative self-fulfilling prophecy.

Self-fulfilling prophecy – if you believe it's going to be a disaster, you're probably right.

The power of the sub-conscious mind can begin to significantly affect our psychological well being in a very negative way. Once a child's filters have been set to notice anything that is potentially dangerous or threatening in both a physical and psychological sense, they start to see all the potential pitfalls in a situation because of the growing self-doubt. The more they visualise a future event where things could perceivably go wrong, then the more likely it is that this will be the final outcome. The net effect of this negative visualisation is that it increases the child's levels of self-doubt to the point where they unconsciously self-sabotage their own efforts without even realising.

Wendy has noticed the effects of negative self-fulfilling prophecy many times in children's approach to their education. One example that demonstrates this concept quite well was a child called Katy. Katy had a very unstable family background. Her mother was a single parent who dropped Katy off at school early, so that she could get to work, and often collected Katy late from the 'After School Club' at the end of the day. Katy frequently worried that her mum might not turn up to collect her at the end of the day. The negative thoughts and self-doubt lowered Katy's confidence and self-esteem, which was reflected in her attitude towards her SATs tests. Despite the fact that she was a bright girl, Katy did not have the confidence to believe she could perform well in her tests. As she once said to Wendy "I'm going to get low scores, so why bother?" Generally Katy performed quite poorly despite the fact that she had the ability to score better. Katy already had a predisposition to view negative DVDs because of her unstable family background. She therefore found it easy to play negative DVD memories of her poor past performance in the tests and this lead her to the conclusion she would perform poorly in future tests.

For Katy to have made a big effort and failed would have been more damaging to her self-esteem than if she made little effort and failed. However, as Wendy noted, the irony is that had Katy made slightly more effort she would almost certainly have scored quite well in the test. Katy just didn't have the confidence to risk the damage to her self-esteem, which was already quite fragile. Katy's case is a complex example of self-sabotage and negative self-fulfilling prophecy.

Thinking errors.
One of the main challenges in combating any kind of psychological distress, and especially depression, is trying to re-set the filter so that it reverses the process i.e. it filters *in* the positive DVD memories and filters *out* the negative ones.

It's quite difficult to do this particularly when a child is experiencing high levels of self-doubt. So what is it that keeps the filter in place so that the negative memories of the past slip into our conscious minds? The answer is that we make what are known as 'Thinking Errors'.

Thinking errors are sub-conscious negative assumptions we make about our world which, when challenged, often prove to be unfounded. David Burns (4) identified some examples of common thinking errors.

1. All or Nothing Thinking. Things are perceived in black or white categories. Anything short of perfection is viewed as a failure.

2. Over Generalisation. A single negative event is perceived as a never-ending pattern of defeat. The word 'always' is often used to describe negative events and 'never' to describe positive events.

3. Mental Filter. Negative events are dwelt on to the exclusion of any positive events. This is described as the drop of ink that discolours the entire glass of water.

4. Disqualifying the Positives. Positive experiences are described as not counting – it was easy, anyone can do that.

5. Jumping to Conclusions. Negative interpretations occur even though there are no facts to support the conclusion e.g. "everyone's got it in for me today."

6. Magnification and Minimisation. Magnifying your own errors or other people's achievements. Minimising your own achievements or other people's errors.

7. Emotional Reason. Assuming that your negative emotions reflect the way things really are.

8. Should Statements. When directed inwards, at oneself, they encourage failure or defeat. When directed at others they encourage anger, frustration and resentment.

9. Labelling and mislabelling. An extreme form of generalisation. Instead of describing an error you attach a negative label to yourself or others e.g. "I'm hopeless." "She is an idiot." "It was the worst day of my life." The language is often highly coloured or emotionally loaded.

10. Personalisation. Seeing yourself or someone else as the cause of some negative external event which, in fact, you or the other person, were not responsible for.

David Burns did a wonderful job of identifying these errors. There seems to be a lot of overlap between his third error – Mental Filter and Rick's theory of how the RAS filter works. We believe that it's the third error that is the **key**, the rest of the thinking errors seem to operate by keeping the mental filter in place. So, for example, with 'should statements' a child focuses only the negative aspect of a DVD memory i.e. what they *didn't* do well in a specific situation, rather than anything positive that they *did* achieve in the same situation.

In Part II of the book many of the exercises are specifically designed to try to help children challenge their thinking errors and therefore allow positive DVDs to get through the filter. Therefore it's vital that we understand the part that thinking errors play in keeping the filter in place thereby causing children to focus mainly on the negative aspects of their lives.

A good example of a child making thinking errors was the case of Bonnie. Bonnie never went in for team sports, such as rounders or netball, because she believed that she was too fat to be successful. Whilst it's true that Bonnie would never be described as slim, she wasn't an obese child who could not do any physical activities. When Wendy chatted to her about this Bonnie quickly made a couple of thinking errors. "I'm hopeless at sport. I'll never be any good. The only kids that are good at sport are all slim and fit." Bonnie was mislabelling herself as 'hopeless' and over generalising with the use of the words 'never' and 'only'. These thinking errors kept Bonnie's filter in place. They made her focus only on her lack of success in certain sports, such as rounders and netball. Wendy was able to challenge Bonnie's thinking errors by showing her a video of women athletes competing in field events such as the discus, shot and javelin. Wendy also invited a disabled athlete in to school to challenge children's negative perceptions and thinking errors.

The following diagram shows the links between playing negative DVDs (negative introspective thought patterns) – the increasing levels of self-doubt – the lack of confidence – low self-esteem – and finally the negative self-fulfilling prophecy. In short, if children constantly have thoughts about their lack of success in the past this increases the likelihood of being unsuccessful in the future: "I never thought it would happen."

The cycle of depression.

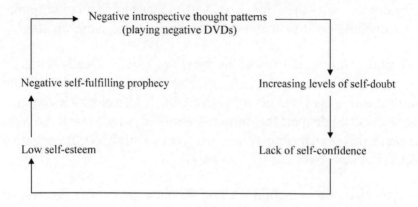

Negative introspective thought patterns
(playing negative DVDs)

Negative self-fulfilling prophecy

Increasing levels of self-doubt

Low self-esteem

Lack of self-confidence

Summary of Chapter 3
I never thought it would happen.

Self-doubt, threat sensitivity, risk aversion and pessimism.
Self doubt can be linked to being threat sensitive i.e. noticing all the potential dangers in life. In turn, this can lead to risk aversion – never doing risky things for fear of the dangers. Ultimately this manifests itself in pessimism – assuming the worst will happen. Some children are predisposed to pessimism because of three factors that were present in their lives when they were younger which made them threat sensitive: a genetic predisposition from anxious parents; some form of abuse; an awareness of a general anxiety-producing situation.

The dangers of pessimism.
Pessimism seems to be linked to poorer health, lower life expectancy, lower levels of success and it's just less fun than being optimistic. Worse than this, it can also lead to children experiencing negative self-fulfilling prophecies.

Self-fulfilling prophecy.
The cycle of repeatedly playing negative DVDs of past events where we judged ourselves as failures begins to impact on the outcome of how we will handle similar situations in the future. A child will believe that they will fail in the future because they have lots of negative DVD evidence to show how they failed in the past. They then create negative DVD memories about possible failures in the future.

Thinking errors.
These are the negative assumptions and conclusions that we draw about others and ourselves. Thinking errors keep the filter firmly in place. They make sure that we focus on negative DVD memories. The negative DVD memories are filtered from the sub-conscious into the conscious mind. The positive DVD memories are left in

the sub-conscious mind and don't register in the conscious mind. As a result of the thinking errors fixing the filter in place, the cycle of self-doubt, lack of confidence, low self-esteem and negative self-fulfilling prophecies occur. So, with the consequent failure, yet another negative DVD is stored in the mind's library, ready to be registered on the conscious mind when it is pushed through the filter.

CHAPTER 4
RUNNING IN THE FAMILY.

So far, we've talked about the changes in society that have occurred in the 21st century and the potential negative impact on children's psychological well being. We've also provided an understanding of how the mind works and the links between playing negative DVDs - thinking errors - increased self-doubt - low self-confidence - negative self-fulfilling prophecy - pessimism - depression. However, it's important to remember that most children experience some difficult times during childhood and adolescence without necessarily falling into the cycle described above. These difficult times are known as 'life events' and in this chapter we'll attempt to explore the connection between life events and children's susceptibility to psychological distress.

Life Events.
Rich or poor, black or white, gay or straight, it is inevitable that all children will experience life events whilst growing up. Life events include situations that are very obviously negative such as parents getting divorced, the death of a close relative, splitting up from a boy/girlfriend or being bullied at school. Equally, even potentially happy events, such as the birth of a sibling, or moving house can also be quite stressful for children. The natural course of life brings children into contact with events that can be psychologically challenging. The effect of life events can mean increasing amounts of psychological distress on the part of the person going through the life event. This is inevitable, as Rick mentioned in 'The Promised Land' (1) - "into every life a little rain must fall."

Earlier in the book we noted that some children are more prone to psychological distress than others and there are three mechanisms through which this susceptibility manifests itself:

1. Through the effects of nature and nurture: threat sensitivity is either genetically inherited or reinforced and nurtured.
2. Through the effects of mental, physical or sexual abuse.
3. By exposure to general anxiety producing situations which persist for a length of time.

Rick's experience of working with adults in a clinical setting suggests that in the region of 75% of his clients have the root of their psychological distress located in this early susceptibility during childhood or adolescence.

All children experience life events but not all succumb to the depressive cycle. On the other hand, some children succumb to depression but don't appear to have any life events to deal with. So why some children and not others? The answer lies internally, in each child's psychological make-up. It is the interaction between their internal psychological make-up and their external world, which defines how well they will deal with life's difficulties. Our explanation for this is 'pegs and holes'. Imagine there is a round hole in the side of a bathtub full of water. If we put a square peg in the hole in an attempt to prevent the water escaping then the water will seep through because the peg doesn't fit the hole.

Each child is unique. They are 'pegs' which are all a slightly different shape to each other; no two pegs are exactly the same. Children's internal psychological make-up makes them the peg shape that they are. This may help them deal with certain aspects of their life very well, but may not help them deal so effectively with other challenges in their lives. For example emotional resilience is a very useful trait in certain situations, such as when a child has to deal with bullying. However, very emotionally resilient children can be insensitive to the needs of others. So, like most traits, it can be an advantage in one situation but potentially a disadvantage in others. Emotional resilience helps explain why some children are better equipped than others to withstand the three mechanisms through which threat sensitivity manifests itself, namely: nature/nurture, abuse and generalised anxiety.

Potential for psychological distress.
The following model suggests that children with relatively low levels of emotional resilience but high levels of threat sensitivity (due to the effects of nature/nurture, abuse or generalised anxiety) will be those who may suffer the most from psychological distress.

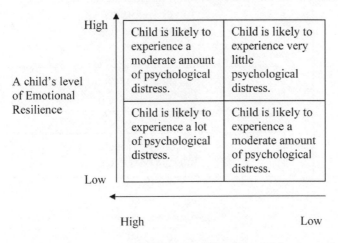

A child's level of Threat Sensitivity due to the effects of nature/nurture, abuse or generalised anxiety in early life.

In order to understand how a child's internal psychological make-up interacts with their external world we need a working model. The following model is Rick's 'Human Factors' model from 'The Promised Land', which attempts to explain how we become the people we are.

The Human Factors Model.

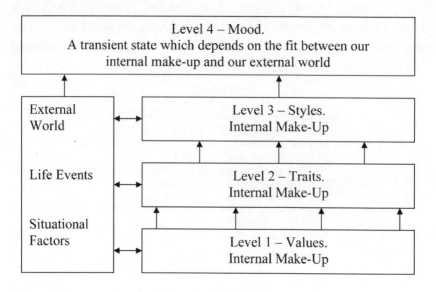

Values.

The building blocks for a child's internal make-up are their values - the first level in the Human Factors Model. These are the beliefs children have about the world around them. Their values give them a code of acceptable conduct about how they should interact with individual people and society as a whole. Their values are represented in the attitudes and behaviours that they strongly embrace.

Where do children get their values? Usually it's a combination of nature and nurture. They inherit some of them directly through their parents, and some of them from the effect of the environment they are exposed to during their formative years. Their values are continually being developed, but by the time they reach their mid to late twenties it appears that they become relatively fixed and enduring. It seems that parents remain highly successful at transmitting values, beliefs, attitudes and aspirations to their children through the process of socialisation (2), particularly when children are relatively young. In teenage years peers may be more influential than parents. Once we reach our mid to late twenties our values don't change much unless, like St Paul on his way to Damascus, we are hit by a bolt of lightning which fundamentally shakes our values and leads us to question them.

Children are forming their values as they grow and develop and this leads to the next level in the model – Traits.

Traits.
Traits are characteristics that can usually be measured using psychometric tests. These characteristics could include, for example:

- Personality traits such as introversion/extroversion (3).
- Strength traits (4) - things we have a natural talent for, such as the ability to think analytically or the ability to bring harmony to a situation.
- Motivational traits, for instance, whether we are motivated by the promise of something good if we do it, or the threat of something bad if we don't (5).

There are various different forms of traits, which interact with, and influence each other. The key thing about traits is that they are the tangible manifestations (demonstrated in the way a child acts and talks) of the internal values they hold dear.

Once again, traits become relatively fixed and enduring by the time we reach our mid to late twenties. However, we can start to see traits develop as children begin to mature and develop.

Style.
The next level in the Human Factors model is described as style. Based on the two previous levels children develop a certain style in terms of the way they typically behave in certain situations. Style is the tangible manifestation of a child's traits and values. There are many measures of different styles, such as learning styles (6).

Some children are active learners and enjoy learning environments where there are lots of opportunities to interact whilst they learn. Other children are reflective learners and prefer learning in a quieter environment where they can observe and think.

Research suggests that those with active learning styles are more likely to have extroversion as a trait, whilst reflective learners are more likely to have introversion as a trait. The predisposition to introversion/extroversion is likely to be influenced by both the genes of the parents and the values instilled in children about how to learn 'best'. Strongly introverted parents will probably enjoy reflective learning situations and may instil the value of this in their children.

Mood.

Mood is at the next level. The difference between mood and the preceding levels is that mood is transitory - it isn't fixed. Even quite seriously depressed people aren't depressed all the time. Sometimes we're happy, sometimes we're sad, and this is likely to be influenced by the external situation we find ourselves in. For most of us, the more a situation suits our values, traits and styles, then the more positive our mood is likely to be – a square peg in a square hole. The less we are suited to the situation i.e. the more challenged we are, then the greater the potential for anxiety, stress and depression. A child who has had the value of physical exercise and sport reinforced by their parents will probably find PE lessons at school quite enjoyable. For children who have neither the values nor traits to enjoy or recognise the importance of PE, then the lesson may be quite a stressful experience. A good example of this is Noel who frequently played truant from school on days when he was supposed to take part in PE or sports.

In the preceding chapter we looked at why some people have a predisposition to being prone to psychological distress. We suggested this was due to threat sensitivity emanating from three factors: nature/nurture; abuse; generalised anxiety. However, these factors alone don't account for why some children become very stressed, anxious or depressed when faced with life events. We also need to take into account a child's internal make-up: their values, traits and styles. These, combined with their levels of threat sensitivity, will probably determine their potential to succumb to psychological distress.

Summary of Chapter 4
Running in the family.

Life events.

These are the significant milestone events that mark our lives. They can be either positive (moving to a new house or the birth of a sibling) or negative (the death of a close relative or parents divorcing) but both have the power to induce a certain amount of distress in children. Children may be more or less susceptible to psychological distress dependent on: the effects of nature/nurture; the effects of abuse; or the exposure to general anxiety producing situations that persist for a length of time. However, another factor that determines how well children deal with life events is the match between their internal make-up and the external challenge.

The Human Factors Model.

Values.

These are the beliefs that children inherit from the effects of both nature and nurture. They tend to be relatively fixed and enduring. They don't change much after we reach a certain age - probably our mid to late 20s. They are the bedrock upon which most of our observable behaviour is built.

Traits.

These are the individual characteristics a child develops throughout their formative years, such as personality traits. Like values, traits seem to be relatively fixed and enduring, although they are influenced to a degree by the situation the child finds themselves in. Traits are also a product of both nature and nurture.

Styles.

These are the tangible summation of a child's values and traits. We can describe a child's style from what we see and hear. We can usually work out some of the traits and values that underpin a child's style. Because styles are based on values and traits, once again they tend to be relatively fixed and enduring. Style demonstrates how a child typically interacts with their external world.

Mood.

Moods are transient - they change according to how well we feel we are equipped to cope with what's going on in our external world. If a child's external world is not a good fit with their internal world then their mood can become depressed. It's important to remember that even clinically depressed people are not depressed all the time - mood is transient, it changes.

CHAPTER 5
BLUNTED ON REALITY.

The myth of weak characters.
Children succumb to the effects of psychological distress because of the way their values, traits and style interact with the prevailing external situation they find themselves in. In short, depression, anxiety and stress are due in part to the child, and in part to the particular circumstances the child finds themselves in.

It's important not to think of children who struggle with life events as being somehow 'weak characters' and those who seem to cope well as being 'strong characters'. However, many people fall into this trap. This is one of the reasons why children who suffer from aspects of psychological distress may get less sympathy than children suffering from an obvious tangible physical ailment. The tendency is to assume that it is the child's inherent inability to cope with their life – the lack of emotional resilience - that is the main reason for their stress, anxiety or depression. Whilst this may play a part, we should not underestimate the difficulty of the circumstances the child may currently find themselves exposed to.

Psychologists call this tendency to attribute the outcome in a situation to the person's response to the situation rather than the situation itself, Fundamental Attribution Error (FAE). The term comes from the research on attribution (1). In the context of depression, anxiety or stress it simply means that we have a tendency to attribute the distressed state of mind to the child's traits rather than attributing it to their circumstances. Most children placed in certain very stressful situations will react in a similar way. However, we have a strong tendency to attribute the child's reaction to the child, rather than the situation. Nisbett and Ross (2) quote many experiments that demonstrate the human tendency to attribute outcomes to the person not the situation.

One classic experiment involved researchers filming two teams of basketball players of very similar ability practising shooting baskets in the school gym. Team 1 practised in a brightly-lit gym and performed very well. Team 2 practised in the same gym but with the lights turned down very low. Not surprisingly team 2 performed much worse.

When the researchers showed the film to groups of subjects and asked them to say which players they thought were the most skilful a significant majority of subjects said team 1. The subjects attributed team 2's failure to perform well to the players rather than the situation i.e. the poorly lit gym. Even when the researchers pointed out the fact to the subjects that team 2 were performing in a poorly lit gym, the subjects still judged team 1 to be more skilful.

Most of us would perform poorly at this task if we were playing in a badly lit gym. By the same token, most people will probably experience psychological distress when they are faced with emotional life events. Unfortunately, if we place too much emphasis on a child's traits it encourages children who succumb to the stress of the life event to believe they are less capable than other children. Fundamental Attribution Error can also result in teachers, childminders and parents mislabelling the child, which can have a damaging effect on the child's self-esteem.

Liam was a child who was experiencing severe stress when faced with the prospect of his mother going to live in Cyprus with his sibling whilst he was left in care. Liam became unmanageable in mainstream schooling and was labelled a 'naughty' child by staff and adults. Other professionals claimed Liam had ODD - oppositional defiant disorder. The natural tendency was for most people to attribute Liam's behaviour to the person, not to the situation Liam found himself in. After much discussion the provision of schooling was changed to allow Liam to work in smaller classes where he was able to receive more attention. However, Liam's self-esteem was highly damaged, not just by the fact that his mother had abandoned him, but also because of the attribution errors made by people around Liam.

A balanced view – changing perceptions.
Rick's role as a psychologist is not to try to change people - it is to help people better understand themselves and the situations they find themselves in. Hopefully, parents, childminders and teachers can take a similar approach to children. Whilst it may be desirable to help nurture children's values traits and styles in a positive direction, we shouldn't try to ignore the effects of nature. Whilst it's a fairly common view that both nature and nurture affect our internal psychological make-up, it's worth remembering that nature gets first bite of the cherry through the genes that each child inherits at birth.

If we can help children to understand how the interplay between their internal world (values, traits and styles) and their external world (life events, situation) can lead to self-doubt, lack of confidence, low self-esteem and ultimately to negative self-fulfilling prophecy, they can begin to move forward. From an enlightened perspective, children will be able to reflect on why they are making the thinking errors, which hold the filter in place so that predominantly negative DVD memories are filtered into their conscious mind. It's not about changing children, it's about helping them to change their perception of themselves and their lives. In essence our job is to help children play more positive DVDs of themselves and their situation so they can begin the process of perceptual change.

Control and letting go.
In the 'Promised Land' Rick tells the following story. Rick was teaching a post-graduate class for American teachers in Ohio USA. As the first session of the class unfolded, one woman who seemed to have quite a forceful, dominant character intrigued Rick. In the discussion the class were having about what made an effective learning environment this woman's views were quite clear on the role that the teacher should play. She seemed a little dismissive of the views of other people in the class who felt that the students should play a part in deciding their own environment. As the temperature rose later in the day, this lady removed her sweatshirt and underneath she wore a tee shirt with the simple message "Because I'm the teacher!"

Believing we can control other people's behaviour because of our position of authority can easily set us up for failure. The reality is that the only person's behaviour we can truly control is our own.

This lesson is as important for children to learn as it is for adults. The more we let go of situations we can't control and channel our energy into what we can control then the better our self-confidence and self-esteem. This makes sense when we think about the analogy in previous chapters about the mind playing DVD memories. If we spend more time on controlling our own behaviour – *and using this as the benchmark for our success* - we will have a store of positive DVD memories in the library. When we re-play the positive memories this helps to combat the self-doubt and increase our self-confidence.

The issue of control is closely linked to the concept of changing our perceptions in order to get a more balanced perspective on our lives, which we discussed earlier. Children are particularly prone to experiencing stress from feeling that they have little or no control over their lives. A good example of how this manifests itself is in the reasons behind eating disorders. The research on anorexia seems to suggest that a child's ability to control how they look through controlling their diet is one of the psychological components in anorexia. Anorexia typically starts in adolescence or early adulthood, and between 5 and 22 percent of patients with eating disorders die or commit suicide (3). Research conducted by Westen and Harnden-Fischer (4) suggests that severe anorexics often have a 'constricted/overcontrolled' personality and have difficulty in acknowledging or expressing anger or their own wishes.

Broadly speaking, the more control we feel we have, then the more positive DVD memories we will store in the library in our mind and the better the balance between positive and negative DVD memories. If we focus on controlling our own behaviour in order to try to influence other people to make positive choices we will experience more success than if we believe we can control other people's behaviour through sheer force of personality.

Many of the psychologically distressed children Wendy has worked with over the years feel quite unable to control their lives. This lack of control is closely linked to the curse of self-doubt, the lack of confidence and the loss of self-esteem we talked about earlier in the book. When children experience psychological distress it's because there is a poor fit between their internal world (values, traits and styles) and their external world (life events, situation). The perceived lack of control that emanates from this poor fit can be a contributory cause to a depressed mood state.

The story of Justin, who we mentioned earlier, helps to demonstrate this. Justin was the thirteen-year-old boy Wendy worked with after he became dependent on cannabis following the separation of his parents during an acrimonious divorce. When his mother began a relationship with the man who later became his stepfather, Justin started to trash his bedroom, self-harm and steal before he was eventually referred for psychological support. Justin was trying to control his parents' divorce and the relationship his mother was having with the man who later became his stepfather. Justin was unable to do this directly so he began to make choices about his own behaviour hoping this might influence the behaviour of the adults in his life. Self-harm and anorexia are two examples of behaviour a child can choose over which the child has a huge amount of control and their parents, childminders and teachers have very little influence.

A classic piece of research on British civil servants (5) suggested that the more control they felt they had over their work then the lower the levels of stress the civil servants experienced. Although this seems a pretty logical conclusion the relationship between control and stress may be slightly more complex. There doesn't appear to be any disagreement with the idea that the more control we have over our lives the less stressed we will feel. However, in Rick's experience as a psychologist, it seems apparent that some people who have relatively little or even no control over a situation feel fairly low levels of distress - providing they can 'let it go'.

The highest levels of stress seem to occur when someone can neither control a situation fully nor let it go. Accepting that we have relatively little control over certain factors in a situation can be very liberating – providing that we then channel our energies into the factors that we can control. The graph below shows how this works.

Stress and Control.

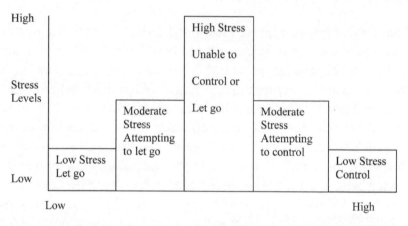

Control Levels

Wendy once worked with a child called Sara who had been abused by a family member. As a result of this, Sara was placed in a home for children. Sara's behaviour towards all adults was very aggressive: she would spit and try to bite teachers at school in an effort to try to exert some control over her situation. Wendy gave Sara a guinea pig to look after whilst she was in the home. By giving Sara responsibility and control of the guinea pig's welfare it allowed her to channel her energies away from something she had not been able to control – the abuse and the resulting placement in the home – into something she could control, the welfare of her pet.

Choices and Consequences.
The idea behind 'choices and consequences' is an important factor in helping to raise children's self-esteem and is linked to the concept of control mentioned above. William Glasser (6) uses the philosophy of

choices and consequences in much of his work. The main principle behind the concept is that we all have choices but if we make poor choices they can lead to negative consequences. It recognises that all of us, including children, have a large degree of free will. Children can make choices about things that involve their own behaviour – they are in control of this. As we mentioned earlier in this chapter psychological distress is closely linked to trying, unsuccessfully, to control situations. The more that children are able to recognise that they have some control over their lives and can influence this control in a positive way then the higher their self-esteem is likely to be.

Self-harm and anorexia are more extreme examples of children's attempts to control and influence adult behaviour. The following story from 'The Promised Land' demonstrates a simple example of choices and consequences.

Eleanor was a client of Rick's who was suffering from depression. Her marriage was in difficulty, the family was experiencing financial hardship and she was struggling to cope with her job. In addition, the biggest difficulty she faced was that her two sons aged nine and eleven were constantly challenging her parenting skills. Although the boys were also experiencing high levels of stress and anxiety, to start with lets look at the story from Eleanor's point of view. Whilst Rick was counselling her she became visibly upset as she described taking her sons to school one day. On arriving outside the school gates both sons refused to get out of the car. The eldest one eventually decided to get out and go into the school playground. However the youngest son, Phillip, simply refused to leave the car. In desperation, Eleanor opened the front passenger door to try to take hold of his arm so she could physically march him onto the school playground.

As she approached the passenger door Phillip jumped across to the driver's seat and hid down by the pedals where his mum couldn't reach him. As Eleanor ran round to the driver's door Phillip jumped back to the other seat and hid on the floor where again she could not reach him. This game of cat and mouse continued for several minutes with Eleanor becoming more and more stressed much to the bemusement of other parents dropping their children off. Eventually she managed to catch hold of Phillip's arm and literally dragged him out of the car. As Eleanor frog-marched him across the playground Phillip threw himself down on the floor and began to shout and scream drawing the attention of the other children and parents to Eleanor's predicament. Eleanor's humiliation was complete when one of the teachers approached her and told Phillip to get up immediately, stop shouting and go into school, a request he complied with straight away.

As Eleanor recounted this story to Rick the tears rolled down her face. She felt a complete failure as a parent when her inability to control her son's behaviour was played out in a very public arena under the gaze of parents and teachers, some of whom expressed quite judgmental views about Eleanor's parenting skills.

"Whose behaviour can you control completely?" Rick asked her. She paused for a long time before replying "Only my own." It can be quite a difficult realisation for many adults to accept that children have a mind of their own, which won't necessarily be influenced by the wishes of parents or teachers.

Teachers and childminders are often more adept at dealing with children who are making poor choices. They have a different relationship with the child and are able to deal more dispassionately with situations such as the one above. To put it simply they don't take it as personally as most parents. Wendy once had to deal with a student who was very aggressive and spat without any provocation. Wendy was able to deal with this in a fairly dispassionate way. She told the student that if he persisted with his behaviour she would have to have him removed from the group because he posed a health hazard due to the problems of bacteria being spread to others from his saliva. Whilst Wendy cared about him as a student she was able to focus on the practical issues because she could remain relatively dispassionate about his behaviour – Wendy knew it wasn't aimed at her.

Let's continue with Eleanor's story. Rick's plan to help Eleanor was fairly simple. Firstly, Eleanor had to accept that she couldn't control her children's behaviour - she could only control her own behaviour. This meant that despite the children's outbursts Eleanor would control her own temper and not rise to the bait. Secondly, Rick asked Eleanor to work out which two or three aspects of the children's behaviour were completely unacceptable. One of these aspects was, not surprisingly, the refusal to go to school. These were to be Eleanor's 'hills worth dying for'. The rest of their behaviour was deemed 'background noise' which was not worth getting into an argument over.

Next, Eleanor would make it absolutely clear to the children that if they chose to ignore Eleanor on the 'hill' issues there would be negative consequences. If they chose to work with her on the hill issues there would be positive consequences. If Eleanor recognised that the children were making 'background noise' she would just ignore the behaviour.

When we first discussed it Eleanor seemed a little uneasy that she should simply ignore some of the children's behaviour. So I asked her how effective, in terms of changing their behaviour, was her current strategy of challenging them on every issue. She paused for a while before she smiled ruefully and admitted that it hadn't succeeded very well. I pointed out to her that it was quite possible that our plan to change their behaviour wouldn't work either, but at least by controlling her own behaviour she wouldn't have the stress and anxiety of the rows.

Eventually, Eleanor began to realise that it was okay to accept that she couldn't control the behaviour of her nine and eleven year-old children completely. However, as long as she controlled her own behaviour she felt calmer and more in control of the situation. This, in turn, allowed her to use the strategy of explaining to the children that it was their decision about whether to choose to behave in an unacceptable way but that their choice would involve certain consequences with regard to future treats.

This example demonstrates beautifully how accepting that we can't control some things allows us to put more energy into affecting what we can control. Eleanor accepted she could not directly control Phillip's behaviour, but by remaining calm and not playing the games that Phillip wanted to engage her in she felt calmer and therefore more able to deal with the situation.

Accepting our limitations and channelling our energies into what we can control makes us feel better. In turn, this allows us to accept our limitations more easily and let go of the things we can't control. Because we are focusing on the positive DVD memories of being in control we have less self-doubt, and our self-esteem and confidence benefit which helps lead to a more positive self-fulfilling prophecy.

The next time Phillip began to play the game of refusing to get out of the car Eleanor's strategy worked very effectively. She had previously explained her problem to Phillip's teacher and warned the teacher that although Phillip might be late for school she wanted the teacher's support to address this problem. The teacher was happy to provide this support when she understood Eleanor's dilemma. Eleanor also pre-warned her boss that she might be a little bit late for work because she was having difficulties with her son but she would happily make the time up. Once again she got a positive response from her boss. This made Eleanor feel more confident and in control before she even arrived at school.

When Phillip began his game of jumping from seat to seat. Eleanor got back into the driver's seat and told Phillip calmly that it was his choice whether he continued to play this game but that she was not prepared to play it with him. She went on to explain why she wanted him to get out of the car and walk into school like the other children and that if he chose not to do this he would not be allowed to play with his friends after school. Phillip initially refused to leave the car and Eleanor said that she thought it was a shame but if he chose not to comply with her request that was his choice, the consequence was that he would not be able to play with his friends. Phillip began to shout and scream that it was unfair. Eleanor calmly picked up her newspaper and started reading it. Eventually Phillip calmed down and when he did Eleanor asked him very politely if he would please get out of the car and walk with her into school. After a few minutes Phillip left the car quietly and Eleanor thanked him as they walked together into school. She also promised him that if he was good about getting out of the car the following day he would be able to play with his friends after school.

Eleanor was able to control her own responses to Phillip's behaviour. She was also able to successfully influence Phillip's teacher and her own boss to support her in dealing with Phillip's behaviour. This increased her feelings of control over the situation. Regardless of how Phillip behaved she would have a positive DVD memory stored of how she successfully controlled her own behaviour and got support from two key people. There are two further potential benefits that can result from this. First, if Eleanor has a difficult day in the future and she loses her patience with Phillip (which will almost certainly happen because she's only human!) she will be able to counter the thinking error that "I never seem to be able to deal calmly with Phillip." She can search her mental DVD library and she will find the positive DVD of her dealing calmly with his temper outburst which will disprove the thinking error that she can't deal calmly with him. Second, she will be better able to break the cycle of pessimistic self-fulfilling prophecy. The confidence she has gained from dealing with Phillip calmly in the past will increase her belief that she can do it successfully again in the future.

But what about Phillip's psychological distress and the effects on his self-esteem? As Eleanor came to understand the concept of choices and consequences more fully she began to discuss the family's difficulties with Phillip. She listened to his thoughts and began to understand why he sometimes behaved in negative ways. She also began to try to increase his sense of control by including him in the decision making process wherever possible. It wasn't always possible to accommodate Phillip's wishes in all the decisions. A good example of this would include the subsequent decision that Eleanor made to get divorced. Initially Phillip was quite upset by this. However by trying to explain the situation and the reasons behind it, this mitigated the psychological distress. At the same time Eleanor made every effort to include Phillip in as many other decisions as she could which further increased his sense of control.

Getting a balanced perspective on control.
In life a balanced perspective is important and finding equilibrium is vital for children to have good psychological health. An understanding of what we can control and what we have very little control over is an example of equilibrium. Sometimes however children suffer from a vicious circle. They play the negative DVDs of the difficulties they may be experiencing in their lives and this leads to the self doubt, lack of confidence and low self-esteem that we mentioned earlier. In turn, however, this can lead to them believing they can't control certain situations where in fact they can. So they start to externalise their lack of success. They put undue emphasis on the external factors in a situation blaming these for their lack of success. In essence this is the reverse of Fundamental Attribution Error! They blame the situation rather than looking at themselves. Externalising has the effect of disempowering children.

Wendy often comes across examples of externalising. A classic case of this is in primary age range children who are labelled 'special needs'. Such children often start to sabotage their whole school experience and blame their special needs label to justify lack of success in every area of their educational experience. Wendy often uses puppets to help motivate these children. As the children become skilled in puppetry they receive a certificate for outstanding work with puppets, which helps to internalise their thinking.

It's important to get the balance right: beating ourselves up over things we can't control increases our sense of failure, but making excuses and blaming other people when we could have influenced a situation disempowers us. So, it's vital to help children to accept what they can't control and channel their energies into what they can control - balance.

Getting a balanced perspective on optimism.

In taking our theme of balance further it's important to look at the concept of optimism again. In the earlier discussion on the brain's filter, the RAS, we noted that when our filter has been set to notice all the negative things in our lives that we lose a balanced perspective. The more a child plays the negative DVD memories, the greater their self-doubt and the less they feel able to control or influence many aspects of their lives. In turn, this can lead to pessimism and negative self-fulfilling prophecy.

However, whilst it's an advantage to be broadly optimistic about life, blind optimism can be quite damaging too - it's not a balanced view of life. Earlier when we demonstrated the model of the filter with black and white DVDs we pointed out the dangers of having our filters set to allow only the black negative DVDs through the filter. However, it's important to recognise that only allowing the white DVDs through the filter also shows a lack of perspective and balance.

In his book, 'Good to Great' (7) Jim Collins talks about the 'Stockdale Paradox', which recognises the importance of acknowledging the brutal truth of a negative situation whilst, at the same time, being broadly optimistic that the situation will improve. The Stockdale Paradox is named after Admiral Stockdale, the highest-ranking officer in the US Navy to be captured by the North Vietnamese during the Vietnam War.

Stockdale noticed that, when first captured, some servicemen were unrealistically optimistic about how soon the war would be over and when they would be repatriated. The psychological well being of these individuals deteriorated very rapidly when time passed and they were still imprisoned. Their initial confidence that "we'll all be home by Christmas" was severely dented when Christmas had come and gone and they were still imprisoned. The servicemen who fared best during their imprisonment were those who faced the brutal truth – that they wouldn't be home by Christmas – but who also never stopped believing that they would eventually be repatriated with their families.

Justin, who we mentioned in Chapter 2, was a good example of not adopting the Stockdale Paradox. Following the acrimonious divorce of his parents, Justin's mother began a relationship with the man who was to eventually become his stepfather. Rather than face up to the 'brutal truth' Justin chose to bury his head in the sand and refused to accept the notion that this man and his mother might eventually marry. Justin began smoking cannabis to help him blot this possibility out of his consciousness. When the realisation that his mother and her partner were going to marry finally dawned on him it came as a real shock and he resorted to a number of very negative behaviours including crime and self-harm. Wendy had to help Justin face up to the brutal truth yet remain optimistic that there were positive outcomes from this scenario.

These examples help to demonstrate the importance of balance. If children are able to get a balanced perspective they can even appreciate the poignancy of very difficult emotional situations and become stronger as a result. They are also able to accept themselves in a much less judgmental way, which decreases their self-doubt and raises their self-esteem.

Summary of Chapter 5
Blunted on reality.

The myth of weak characters.
Some children seem to cope better with life events than others. However, this does not make some children 'strong' characters and others 'weak' characters. It seems that generally we have a desire to want to explain a person's success or failure in coping with a particular situation by attributing it to the individual rather than accepting that the situation itself may have had a big part in deciding the outcome. Fundamental Attribution Error (FAE) is the name given to this phenomenon. Most people placed in difficult, challenging situations would probably respond in a broadly similar fashion – they would all experience a degree of stress.

A balanced view – changing perceptions.
Helping children with psychological distress is about providing them with the tools to change their perception of themselves and their lives: the interplay between their internal and external worlds. It's not about fundamentally changing them as individuals. We are who we are. To understand ourselves better makes us more accepting of our internal world and our ability to relate to the external world.

The concept of control.
Traditional thought suggests that the more control we have over a situation the less stress or anxiety we experience. This may be a view that is over simplified. It is possible to have low levels of control *and* low levels of stress if we can accept that there are some things we can't control and we channel our energies into controlling the factors that can be controlled. By helping children to focus on what they can control this leads to positive DVDs being played and an increase in their self-confidence. Helping children to understand that some factors in a situation can't be controlled avoids the self-doubt that can creep in when they view themselves in the context of thinking errors. This is summed up by the thinking error on Personalisation, that is, 'seeing yourself or someone else as the

cause of some negative external event which the individual was not responsible for'.

Choices and Consequences.
The main principle behind this concept is that we all have choices, but if we make poor choices they can lead to negative consequences. It recognises that all of us, including children, have a large degree of free will and they can make choices about things that involve their own behaviour – they are in control of this. However, this concept also accepts that other people also have choices about how they behave and that all we can do is try to influence other people's choices through controlling our own behaviour. Helping children to understand that there are potential positive and negative consequences for their behaviour helps them to make better choices.

Getting a balanced perspective on control.
Making every effort to control what we genuinely can control leads to internalising our attribution and can empower us. However, it's important to get the balance right: beating ourselves up over things we can't control increases our sense of failure. However, making excuses and blaming other people when we could have influenced a situation disempowers us. Helping children to distinguish between what they can and can't control allows them to channel their energies appropriately.

Getting a balanced perspective on optimism.
Whilst the dangers of pessimism are well documented, blind optimism can be almost as dangerous. The Stockdale Paradox sums this up neatly: help children to face up to the brutal truth in a situation, but at the same time help them to remain broadly optimistic that if they focus on what they can control, the situation will eventually turn out positively.

CHAPTER 6
UNDER PRESSURE.

So far this book has tried to provide an explanation of what happens in the mind of a child who is suffering from some form of psychological distress. We have looked at the links between thinking errors and the filter causing negative DVD memories to predominate in the form of negative introspection, which subsequently leads to self-doubt, lack of confidence, low self-esteem and negative self-fulfilling prophecy. This chapter will look at why our mind goes through this process and in particular, how it reacts to very traumatic life events in order to try to protect us in the short-term. Whilst this book isn't designed to deal in depth with childhood trauma it helps to have a basic understanding of how the mind functions when faced with deeply unpleasant situations.

The mind's immune system.
A child's mind is a very complex and powerful piece of equipment. Whenever children are emotionally troubled the mind automatically tries to help them get through their difficulties. In a similar way to the physiological immune system, the mind works to help protect us against our emotional troubles. However, it seems that the mind's immune system is programmed for short-term protection rather than long-term solutions. When we experience emotionally difficult times our conscious mind is alerted to look out for potentially threatening situations. This occurs because of our sensitivity to negative DVD memories from the past, which have been allowed through the filter from the sub-conscious mind.

The case of Jackie, a young woman who Rick worked with, is a good example of short-term protection rather than long-term solutions. When Jackie was a teenager her parents drank quite heavily and frequently rowed with each other. Often these rows would end up with her parents physically fighting each other, with Jackie occasionally caught in the crossfire. Jackie recalled many times when she was walking home from school wondering what the evening would bring. When she got home she would look for signs from her parents as to what mood they were in, whether they had been drinking and how they spoke to each other. She became quite skilled at spotting the cues that would inevitably lead to violent arguments and often she was able to leave the house before the rows escalated into violence. Unfortunately for Jackie, her filter had been set so effectively to enable her conscious mind to actively look for the danger signals from her parents' behaviour that it generalised Jackie's pattern of thinking.

Jackie became very threat sensitive and began to make negative assumptions about the dangers in life generally. This thinking error caused Jackie to look for all the negative things in her life – her filter was set early in her life to notice the negatives. This thought pattern continued for many years after she left home and no longer needed to be aware of the potential threats from her parents' violent rows. The immune system strategy may have worked in the short-term, but not in the long-term.

Another aspect of the sub-conscious mind trying to help children through their emotional difficulties occurs when they are faced with traumatic life events. Sometimes, the only way they feel they can deal with a very painful event is *not* to deal with it. When we are in shock over something incredibly painful our mind operates in a radically different way to help us cope. The immune system detects the DVD memory responsible for the pain and isolates it in a part of the mind's DVD library. In effect, it puts the memory into quarantine. In 'The Promised Land' Rick likens this to the DVD being placed in a box and a heavy weight put on the lid of the box to prevent it from springing open.

Keeping the lid on the box.
Tina came from a family of four brothers and two sisters. When she was eight years old she was sexually abused by one of her brothers who was six years older than her. This abuse continued until she was fourteen when the elder brother left home. Tina never told anyone about it because she felt so ashamed of what happened to her.

Eventually, in her late teens, Tina formed a relationship with a man who she eventually married, although she never mentioned the sexual abuse to her husband. Soon after the marriage Tina found out that her husband had a drink problem and he began to physically abuse Tina when she became pregnant with their child. After two years of marriage Tina left her husband and filed for divorce. In her early twenties Tina decided that she simply did not want another relationship with a man. She continued to keep the secret of the sexual abuse and also decided to make a secret of the physical abuse she endured at the hands of her ex-husband.

Not only did Tina never tell anyone about what happened to her, she didn't even acknowledge it to herself. She took those particularly painful DVD memories of the abuse and put them in a box on a high shelf in the DVD library in her mind. Tina then put a heavy weight on the box to make sure it didn't spring open. The DVDs were in quarantine and Tina didn't want to let those incredibly powerful negative memories 'infect' the rest of her mind

If Tina never looked at those DVD memories she could pretend they didn't happen. The technique proved quite successful, at least up to a point. For the next 15 years she never once spoke about the abuse or acknowledged that it happened. Then she met Mike. Tina had no intention of forming another relationship with a man. She and her daughter were quite happy together, but a chance meeting with Mike started a friendship and Tina realised she was beginning to have very deep feelings for him. As the relationship became more intimate, the DVD memories forced their way out of the box. Once the DVD memories were out of the box she had great difficulty not playing them over in her mind. Not surprisingly, the more she played the DVDs, the more they 'infected' her mind and she became anxious, distressed and depressed in a fairly short period of time.

Tina soon realised that she had to confront those DVDs with professional support and eventually she was able to lay the ghost of those memories. She no longer had to keep the DVDs in a box with a weight on it. She was simply able to put the DVD away in the library and choose not to go there, whilst, at the same time, knowing that if the DVDs were inadvertently triggered they no longer had the same power to bring on the symptoms of stress, anxiety and depression.

As I mentioned earlier, the technique of quarantining the DVD memory in the box and securing it with a heavy weight was successful up to a point for Tina. However, there was a cost for her. For many years she simply avoided any meaningful contact with men, fearful that any type of relationship would trigger the box to spring open and play the painful DVD memories of the abuse. In this area of her life she became emotionally stunted as she robbed herself of potentially fulfilling relationships which might have brought her a raft of positive emotions.

Keeping the lid on the box is hard work. Ensuring the heavy weight stays in place to make certain the box doesn't fly open takes a lot of effort. All this effort reinforces the fact that there is a box of negative DVD memories in the library ready to infect the sufferer's mind if the lid flies open. The person's sub-conscious mind becomes acutely aware of this negative aspect of their life quarantined in the box. In turn, this prompts the filter to keep searching for dangerous triggers that could cause the box to spring open. In Tina's case this involved self-sabotage. Tina made herself deliberately unattractive to men and ruthlessly quashed any chance of a potential relationship. It was only when Mike somehow 'sneaked under her radar' that she knew she had to confront the problem.

Lifting the lid off the box.
It's only by deliberately and gradually releasing the lid of the box that we can start to come to terms with traumatic life events. In an ideal situation a good counsellor can help to do this. Even talking

to close supportive friends, relatives or teachers, who won't judge, blame or offer well meaning, but perhaps inappropriate advice, can help to gradually open the box. To use the immune system analogy, releasing the lid of the box gently is like allowing some anti-bodies into our mind so we can gradually build up our immunity.

The earlier we can help children to deal with a trauma the better. Many things can be quite traumatic to children. Shakira who we mentioned in Chapter 2 was seriously bullied at school. The bullying also involved violence and left her literally rigid with fear. Fortunately, Shakira was able to share her experiences with Wendy and was able to start to come to terms with what happened to her. Had Shakira placed the DVDs in a box and not been able to deal with them the effects may have surfaced many years later.

In Chapter 2 we also mentioned the case of Graham, who was regularly beaten by all his family members. Graham went through the routine of putting the DVDs in the box and securing it with a heavy weight. Graham developed a particularly clever technique for ensuring he did not view the DVDs: he was able to lose himself in wonderful fantasies, imagining he lived another much happier life. However, he was not as fortunate as Shakira in finding someone who could help him early on and Graham frequently self-harmed as a teenager and young adult.

Knowing how the mind works helps us to be proactive in trying to develop support systems for ensuring that children are not forced to put the painful, unhappy DVDs in a box, which will later become a major block to their self-confidence and self-esteem. However, helping children to talk about deeply upsetting experiences may not be easy. Most children understand intuitively that blocking out painful experiences can be an effective short-term technique for avoiding the pain. But, by leaving the door open for them it allows children the option to walk through it when they are no longer able to keep the lid on the box.

Summary of Chapter 6
Under pressure.

The mind's immune system.
When we experience emotionally difficult times the mind seems to have its own immune system. The conscious mind is constantly on the lookout for potentially threatening situations because of its sensitivity to negative memories from the past that have been allowed through the filter from the sub-conscious mind.

The second aspect of the immune system analogy relates to particularly traumatic life events that are very painful. In this instance, it seems as if these particular DVD memories are placed in a box and a heavy weight is put on the lid. The box is then quarantined in a part of the mind's DVD library, never to be visited.

Keeping the lid on the box.
By quarantining the box it is possible for a child to avoid much of the fear, anger, sadness and sorrow that go with viewing a distressing DVD. If the child never watches the DVD they won't have to deal with the painful emotions. However, it seems that this can make the child emotionally stunted later on in life. Unwilling, or unable, to deal with the negative emotions they can become less able to experience the positive emotions in life.

Lifting the lid off the box.
By slowly lifting the lid off the box it is as if we release anti-bodies into our mind which help us to gradually play the painful DVD and cope with the fear, anger, sadness and sorrow that initially accompanies the DVD. When children face up to their negative emotions they are able to feel more positive and hopeful about the future. Offering children an opportunity to talk about their painful experiences can avoid these DVD memories being consigned to a box with a heavy weight on top.

CHAPTER 7
THE ROAD TO POSITIVE THINKING.

Reasons to be sad: parts one, two and three.
Before we begin to discuss how we can help children start to acquire the habit of positive thinking let's re-cap on why children may be experiencing psychological distress in the first place. Every child, even the most confident and positive individual has the potential to have their filters temporarily set to notice the negative things in their lives. This is likely to occur if they are experiencing a specific life event, such as the death of a close relative, or the divorce of their parents. However, there are three different reasons why children may develop a *predisposition* to thinking negatively and all are related to threat sensitivity.

The first reason is that some children have a predisposition to having their filter negatively set because their parents were very pessimistic abut life. It's possible for parents to transfer this pessimism to their children through either their genes or from constantly reinforcing certain messages about how dangerous and difficult the world is. Many parents are overly protective of their family and can be overheard telling their children to be careful or advising them not to do certain things that are perceived as risky. Whilst it makes sense not to take unnecessary risks, the net effect of constantly pointing out potential threats is that it sets a child's filter to notice the negative things early on in life – the child becomes threat sensitive. It also sub-consciously suggests to the child that the parent doesn't have much confidence in their child's ability to deal with their world effectively, thereby sowing the seeds of self-doubt. Earlier we gave the example of young Sajeed who compulsively rearranged his school equipment on his desk for fear that it would be stolen. Sajeed's mum was very anxious about his safety and she reinforced this message to the lad at every opportunity.

The second reason is that someone may have experienced a very traumatic event or some form of abuse, either in childhood or early adult life that resulted in their filter becoming set to notice negative DVD memories. Jackie's experience, described in the previous chapter, is a good example of this. The bitter and often violent relationship between Jackie's parents undoubtedly made her anxious about her present situation and her immediate and long-term future.

The third reason that some children develop a predisposition to pessimism is because they experience a difficult period in childhood, which involves events that make them anxious about their immediate future. This could be in the form of a life event that occupies a longer period of time in the child's life or it could be the development of a generalised, less specific anxiety. In Chapter 3 we mentioned Katy the ten-year-old girl who began to become very anxious when she was at school. Her mum was a single parent who had recently begun working in a job which meant that she had to pick up Katy from the after school club. Katy's mum was often late and Katy was frequently the last child to be picked up from the club. Katy worried about what might have happened to her mum and whether she would be picked up at all.

In a sense it doesn't matter why a child has become psychological distressed. A similar process is occurring in each of the reasons listed above. The filter has been set to allow negative DVDs from the sub-conscious into the conscious mind and it is the thinking errors that keep the filter in place. The effect of viewing these DVDs regularly over a period of time can cause neuro-physiological changes in the neurotransmitters of the child's brain, particularly in the reduced levels of serotonin and norepinephrine. The effect of viewing these DVDs is psychologically debilitating - self-doubt creeps in, confidence ebbs away and ultimately there is a loss of self-esteem which leads to negative self-fulfilling prophecies and the child becomes stressed, anxious and, quite possibly, depressed.

It's probably true that the more traumatic the root cause in setting the filter, and the longer the child has had their filter set in that position, then the more difficult it is to re-set the filter to notice the positive DVDs. In the last chapter we described the way the mind operates in situations where a child suffers a real shock to their emotional system. After a powerfully traumatic incident some people find the process of re-setting the filter too painful and too much hard work. No technique comes with a guarantee of success. However, the techniques we're going to describe in the next part of the book have enabled us to help hundreds of children and adults to re-set their filters and live happier lives.

Practice makes permanent.
In his book, 'Psycho-cybernetics', Maxwell Maltz (1) suggests that happiness is a habit. There aren't any short cuts to beating psychological distress. We wish there were a simple list of tips that could be implemented effortlessly so that the problem of lack of confidence and low self-esteem could be instantly cured forever. Unfortunately our mind doesn't work like that. Even when prescribed quite powerful anti-depressants it usually takes weeks before the drugs fully take effect – and even then the drugs don't work for everyone. It's also worth remembering that the drugs only affect the symptoms – the chemical imbalance of the neurotransmitters - not the cause, which is the negative introspective thinking cycle.

The rest of this book describes how to use certain strategies and techniques to help children change their thinking. The changes we need to make are linked to conquering the thinking errors. The thinking errors hold the filter in place which, in turn, allows the negative DVDs into our conscious mind and keeps the positive DVDs in our subconscious.

You can either let your mind control you, or you can control your mind - it's a fairly simple choice. The change in thinking only comes with practice, we have to train our minds. In many ways it's like physical training. If you decide you want to become physically fitter and you begin your training programme gradually, after a while you find you're able to do more and you also find that the training becomes easier. After several weeks or months you may have reached your desired level of physical fitness, but you can't stop training and hope that your fitness level will remain constant. However, if you keep up a certain level of training it becomes increasingly easier to fit the training into your life. In fact, you start to miss it when you don't train. It's the same with positive thinking.

If we can help children regularly practice the strategies for making happiness a habit they will reap the benefits, but it requires effort and commitment – and that's something that only you, and the children you care for, can provide. The good news is that practice makes permanent. If we get into these good habits then this new way of thinking eventually marks a permanent change in our perception of life. You will find that you and the children you are helping become more balanced in the way you perceive the world. You will achieve the elusive equilibrium between control and letting go, and the balance between blind optimism and pessimism.

Mental Fitness Training.
We've spent some time understanding the theory of how the mind works, now it's time to explain how we can start to train children's minds to think more positively. As we intimated earlier, the rewards of self-confidence and self-esteem are hard won. Just as a physical fitness programme has to be introduced gently, increased steadily and maintained regularly so it is with mental fitness training. Over the next few chapters we are going to introduce you to a range of mental fitness training techniques for helping children to think positively. The techniques are broken down into five categories:

1. Warm-up activities - these are intended to be the equivalent of helping to stretch a child's mind gently so that we can start the process of challenging their current negative perception of themselves and their world.

2. Jogging – the purpose of these techniques is to make children work a little harder in the shorter term to notice the positive things in their life both in the present and the immediate future.

3. Long steady runs – these activities are designed for helping to create long term positive influences which enhance children's positive perceptions of themselves and their world.

4. Short sprints – these techniques are useful for dealing with potentially more difficult and challenging specific situations. Just like its physical counterpart, a mental sprint is more intense in nature.

5. Warm-down activities – when children have done the hard work it's good to encourage them to have another stretch to reinforce the positive thoughts going forward into the future.

The techniques we are going to describe are designed to challenge the thinking errors, because these are what keep the filters in place. So, let's just refresh our memory of the thinking errors:

All or Nothing Thinking. Things are perceived in black or white categories. Anything short of perfection is viewed as a failure.

Over Generalisation. A single negative event is perceived as a never-ending pattern of defeat. The word 'always' is often used to describe negative events and 'never' to describe positive events.

Disqualifying the Positives. Positive experiences are described as not counting – it was easy, anyone can do that.

Jumping to Conclusions. Negative interpretations occur even though there are no facts to support the conclusion, e.g. "everyone's got it in for me today."

Magnification and Minimisation. Magnifying your own errors or other people's achievements. Minimising your own achievements or other people's errors.

Emotional Reason. Assuming that your negative emotions reflect the way things really are.

Should Statements. When directed inwards, at oneself, they encourage failure or defeat. When directed at others they encourage anger, frustration and resentment.

Labelling and mislabelling. An extreme form of generalisation. Instead of describing an error you attach a negative label to yourself or others, e.g. "I'm hopeless." "She is an idiot." "It was the worst day of my life." The language is often highly coloured or emotionally loaded.

Personalisation. Seeing yourself or someone else as the cause of some negative external event which, in fact, you or the other person, were not responsible for.

As you read the next few chapters, which describe the mental fitness training techniques in detail, keep the thinking errors in mind. Most children who suffer from lack of confidence and low self-esteem have been making thinking errors for months, if not years. Therefore, it's important not to have unrealistic expectations of how quickly the mental fitness programme will take before it begins to make a significant difference. We have found that in general it takes about six to twelve weeks of regular practice before the habit of happiness is gradually acquired. With a combination of effort and support these techniques will work for the vast majority of children, and once the habit has been acquired it's difficult to break!

Summary of Chapter 7
The Road to Positive Thinking.

Reasons to be sad: parts one, two and three.

Every child, even the most confident and positive, has the potential to have their filters temporarily set to notice the negative things in their lives. This is likely to occur if they are experiencing a specific life event. However, there are three basic reasons why children might have a *predisposition* to filter negative DVDs from the sub-conscious into the conscious mind. If this occurs early enough in life it can lead to some children developing the trait of pessimism. The three reasons are:

1. If the child's parents were very pessimistic about life. It's possible for parents to transfer this pessimism to their offspring through either their genes or from constantly reinforcing certain messages about how dangerous and difficult the world is.
2. An individual may have experienced a very specific traumatic event, either in childhood or early adult life that resulted in their filter becoming set to notice negative DVD memories.
3. Some children develop a predisposition to pessimism because they experienced a difficult period in childhood, which involved events that made them generally anxious about their future.

Practice makes permanent.

The filter is kept in place by thinking errors and it's only by continually challenging the thinking errors that we are able to help children to re-set their filters to allow more positive DVD thoughts into their conscious mind. It's hard work. There aren't any short cuts to challenging the thinking errors and it's like physical training: if you stop challenging the thinking errors the negative filter will slip back in place. The good news is that very often you don't have to do anything else apart from challenging the thinking errors. Once the filter is adjusted we start to notice the good things that are already there in our lives.

Mental Fitness Training.

Increasing a child's self-confidence and self-esteem is not an easy task. Like a physical fitness programme, a mental fitness programme has to be introduced gently, increased steadily and maintained regularly. The range of training techniques for helping children to get mentally fit are broken down into five categories:

1. Warm-up activities - these stretch a child's mind gently so that we can start the process of challenging their current negative perceptions.
2. Jogging – these exercises make children work a little harder at noticing the positive things in life, both in the present and the immediate future.
3. Long steady runs – these activities create long term positive influences.
4. Short sprints – these techniques are useful for dealing with potentially more difficult and challenging specific situations.
5. Warm-down activities – these are another series of stretches to reinforce the positive thoughts.

Part II

Changing children's thinking patterns.

CHAPTER 8
WARM-UP ACTIVITIES.

The goal of warm-up activities is to gently stretch the child's mind by challenging any negative assumptions. As Oliver Wendell Holmes Jr once said "A mind once stretched by a new idea never returns to its original dimensions." The warm-up activities are the building blocks for mental fitness and we'll keep returning to them throughout our training programme.

The DVD Library.
It depends on the age of the child, but for most children the simplest warm-up activity can be to explain how their mind works by using the analogy of the DVD library. To re-cap briefly - our memories are stored in the mind as a library full of DVDs. We also create DVD 'memories' about what the future might look like – these are based in large part on our experience of DVD memories of the past. The library is full of both positive and negative DVDs. The negative thinking cycle explains how children can have their filters set to notice all the negative DVDs if they make thinking errors. Constantly viewing negative DVDs leads to self-doubt, lack of confidence, low self-esteem and negative self-fulfilling prophecy.

We've spent quite a lot of time describing this in previous chapters but it is important to help children understand what they are going through. The use of examples and stories of children who have had to deal with similar problems also reassures psychologically distressed children. To help children understand the filter, utilise the example we mentioned in Chapter 2 of the book about red and silver cars.

When explaining the negative thinking cycle it helps to use pictures and diagrams. Later on it can also be very useful for older children to have the list of thinking errors which will help them to become more aware of their current thought patterns.

Make use of the materials in this book to help explain what's going on in the child's mind. 'Knowledge is power'. Understanding *how* the mind works is the first step on the way to making the mind work more effectively.

Reflective Listening.

Our second warm-up activity is designed to help children listen to their own thoughts in order to encourage them to challenge their thinking errors. The listener literally reflects back to the child what they have said in order to get them to think more deeply about their thoughts. Reflective listening involves the listener in asking questions about what the child has just said, rather than making statements.

Rick's son, Jack, is a good artist. Jack has been keen on drawing since he was very young. One day he was trying to draw a difficult landscape and he got very despondent at his lack of success. Rick asked him what the matter was.

"I'm rubbish at art. I just can't do it anymore."

Rick bit his tongue, as he was about to tell Jack how silly his statement was. Rick knew Jack was a good artist but making that statement wouldn't necessarily help Jack.

Instead, Rick asked "What makes you think you're no good anymore?"

He replied "My friend Charlotte is really good at drawing landscapes and I just can't do them."

"Charlotte is a pretty good artist." Rick agreed "Who would you say are the best kids at art in your class?"

"Charlotte, Ellie and Dan are all good."

"What sort of grades did they get in their report cards for art?" Rick asked.

"They all got good grades." Jack replied.

"What did your art teacher say about your ability in your report card?"

"Well I got a good grade too, but I just can't do this stuff. It's much harder and I'm no good anymore."

"What makes drawing landscapes so hard?" Rick quizzed his son.

"It's really hard to get everything in perspective." Jack was adamant about this.

"What do you like drawing best?" Rick asked.

"Cartoon characters." Jack replied.

"I think your cartoon characters are great Jack."

"Yes, but anyone can draw cartoon characters, they're easy!" Jack retorted.

"How many of your friends can draw cartoon characters as well as you?"

"Not many. In fact I'm probably one of the best at cartoon characters." Eventually Jack was starting to change his perception of his artistic ability.

Rick decided to share his own weakness as a writer of novels with Jack. "I've written some books and articles about helping people to think more positively, but I'm not so good at writing stories. I'd love to write a good novel but I just don't have that kind of style. I don't mind though, I get a lot of satisfaction out of writing the other type of books and that more than makes up for not having the talent to write a novel."

Jack smiled "I am pretty good at cartoon characters, and I really like doing them, so maybe it's okay if I'm not great at landscapes, I suppose you can't be good at everything."

As Wendy points out, parents are often not very good at reflective listening with their own children. They think it's quicker and easier to simply explain their own view of the world to a child. However, that's often not the most effective way of changing a child's perception of their world. It would have been much quicker to say to Jack "Don't worry Jack it doesn't matter if you're no good at landscapes because you're great at drawing cartoons." But this wouldn't have necessarily got him to challenge his thinking errors. If you go back to the list of thinking errors you'll see that Jack was guilty of several errors in his thinking including all or nothing thinking, mislabelling himself and disqualifying the positives.

So how can we get better at reflective thinking? The first principle is to listen non-judgementally to what the child is saying. It's very easy to inadvertently put down a child because we have our own strong opinions of life based on our greater experience of the world. We also love our children and want to try to get them to see things from our perspective because we want to quickly ease their pain and soothe their anger. However, if the objective is to increase children's confidence and self-esteem we need to help instil the belief in them that they can solve their own problems. Reflective listening treats them more like an equal and less like a child which then helps change the perception of themselves as more capable individuals.

The second principle of reflective listening is to reflect their thoughts back to them in the form of an open question in order to help them think more critically. Open questions often start with 'What', 'Why', 'Who', 'Where', 'When' or 'How' (sometimes referred to as 5WH). Unlike closed questions – which can be answered with a yes or no – an open question demands more thought in order to answer it.

On a continuum of Open to Closed with the most Open questions to the left, it looks like this:

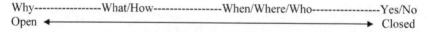

Why-----------------What/How-----------------When/Where/Who-----------------Yes/No
Open ◄――――――――――――――――――――――――――――――――► Closed

'Why' is the most open question because it demands a justification. However it's best not to overdo 'why' questions as they can be a little threatening and sometimes imply that the child did something wrong. "What were your reasons for doing x?" is probably a gentler question than "Why did you do x?"

'What' and 'How' also require higher levels of reasoning in order to answer them properly. 'When', 'Where' and 'Who' questions demand some thought, but the answers are fairly specific. Many Yes/No questions imply that there is a right answer and don't allow the child to think things through themselves. For example: "Wouldn't it be better if you did x?" is really the statement "I think it would be better if you did x" dressed up as a question. A more open question which would allow a child to do their own thinking would be "What would be a better way of doing it?" or "How could you do it better?" You never know, the child might even come up with something you hadn't thought of!

The third principle of reflective listening is making question and answer links. Michael Parkinson, the television interviewer, was very adept at this. He made good question and answer links, and consequently he got his guests to talk quite deeply about various subjects.

Parkinson would ask a question and then listen to the answer, which he used to form the next question. He then listened to the next answer and again used it to formulate the next question. He repeated the process until he felt that a particular line of questioning had been exhausted, then he started another line of questioning. Visually it looks like this:

Using question and answer links is very reaffirming for a child because it demonstrates that you have been really listening to their previous answer. It also allows them to drill down and think more deeply. The child begins to challenge their own thinking errors and suddenly more positive DVDs push through the filter. In the earlier example, Jack's perception of himself as a capable artist was confirmed when he pictured himself drawing cartoons rather than landscapes.

An important addition to reflective listening is to make sure we listen actively. Active listening is about showing a child who is talking to you that you are actually listening to them. Making eye contact and nodding your head are non-verbal clues that indicate we are actively listening to a child who is speaking. Verbal clues include saying things like 'Yes', 'Uh-huh' or 'Okay' which all actively indicate that we are following the child's conversation.

Positive Lists.
A third warm-up exercise is getting children to make positive lists. Again the object is to gently stretch the child's mind so that they challenge the thinking errors by pushing positive DVDs through the filter. Lack of confidence and low self-esteem are built on the premise that the child is no good at anything and is not a worthy person. Creating a positive list challenges this premise.

Ask the child to make a list of 20 positive things in their lives. It helps to give the following examples of the type of things that a child could include in their list: things they are good at, activities they enjoy; friends and family who care about them; achievements they are proud of, things that make them laugh.

A typical list might have the following thoughts:

Scoring a goal for the school team; my cat Fred; raising money from a sponsored swim; the Simpsons TV show; my mum and dad; when I went to Disneyworld; helping my younger sister learn to ride a bike; my best mate Ally; being in the school play; designing my own website; banana milkshakes; listening to my favourite band; getting a grade A for history at school.

There aren't any right or wrong answers for this exercise. The point of the listing exercise is to deliberately get children back into the habit of thinking positively. By expressly asking them to trawl the shelves of their DVD library to find positive thoughts we are getting them to practice the habit of happiness. In effect, the thinking errors ("I'm no good at anything" and "I'm not a worthy person") are being challenged. Once the filter is shifted, the positive memories are pushed from the subconscious mind into the conscious mind.

Sometimes children experiencing high levels of psychological distress can feel overwhelmed by the idea of coming up with a list of 20 positive memories simply because they are very out of practice. The solution to this is to try to do three a day for a week. Get them to keep the list in a notebook. The list then becomes a useful reference to help jog the positive memories when the negative DVDs start to weigh heavily on their mind. Suggesting that the child keeps the notebook by their bedside and recalls three positive memories each night can be a useful way of completing this exercise. There are a number of benefits in doing the exercise this way. First, as we suggested earlier, it's easier to do the exercise in bitesize chunks. Second, the cumulative effect of little and often starts to become habit forming. Third, playing these positive DVDs last thing at night can be a pleasant way to drop off to sleep and, because we are more in tune with our sub-conscious mind during sleep, it can also lead to sweeter dreams!

Writing a list of positive memories in a notebook helps children to see their lives, literally, through a different filter. Their levels of self-doubt decrease as they play DVDs of doing enjoyable activities that they have a talent for. The self-confidence starts to return when they think of their achievements and qualifications. They come to like themselves more and their self-esteem improves as they play the memories of family and friends for whom they have a mutual love and respect for.

We can reinforce the power of these positive DVDs by using the reflective listening techniques as we listen to a child recite their positive list. "What was it you particularly enjoyed about being in the school play?" Or "How did you teach your sister to ride her bike?" Or "What is it about you that your best mate Ally likes?" Many children keep adding to their positive list for years to come. Keeping a scrapbook is a very similar activity and it also has the benefits of utilising visual cues such as a ticket stub from a sports fixture or an achievement certificate to help trigger the memories.

Typically, most children eventually manage to come up with some very effective positive memories from the past. However, sometimes they comment on the fact that many of these memories are about the past rather than the present. Positive listing is a good exercise, but we need to take it a stage further. To achieve this we need a different type of exercise. Having finished our warm-up activities we need to start jogging.

Summary of Chapter 8
Warm-up activities.

The DVD Library.

The simplest warm-up activity is to explain how the mind works by using the analogy of the DVD library. Our memories are stored in the mind as a library full of DVDs. We also create DVD 'memories' about what the future might look like based, in large part, on our experience of DVD memories of the past. The library is full of both positive and negative DVDs. The negative thinking cycle explains how children can have their filters set to notice all the negative DVDs if they make thinking errors. Constantly viewing negative DVDs leads to self-doubt, lack of confidence, low self-esteem and negative self-fulfilling prophecy.

Reflective Listening.

The listener literally reflects back to the child what they have said in order to get them to think more deeply about their thoughts. Reflective listening involves the listener in asking questions about what the child has just said, rather than making statements. The three main principles are:

1. Listen in a non-judgemental fashion without giving an opinion. Treat the child as someone who is capable of solving their own problem with some support.
2. Use open questions to help the child think more critically (5WH).
3. Use question and answer links to help the child's train of thought. Subsequent questions are formulated on the basis of the previous answer.

Positive Listing Exercise.

The negative filter has operated for so long and so effectively that for many children they are simply out of practice in allowing the positive DVDs through the filter and into their conscious mind. By

---

completing a list of positive experiences children begin to practice challenging the thinking errors ("I'm no good at anything" and "I'm not a worthy person") and they start to re-set the filter.

CHAPTER 9
JOGGING.

Jogging builds on the practice of looking at positive DVDs of past events by extending this to looking for positive DVDs in both the present and the immediate future. If we can do this then we can help children to feel more optimistic and hopeful about their current situation and the immediate future.

Catch the moment.
Good things are around us all the time, but when we're stressed, anxious or depressed our filters simply don't allow the good things to make it from our sub-conscious mind into our conscious mind. The wonder of nature, small acts of kindness, beautiful music, the scent of flowers, children's laughter, overcoming life's little challenges, church bells, human touch - all of these can go unnoticed if we let them. Catching the moment is designed to encourage children to notice the good things in their lives by providing a commentary to the DVD *as it's being recorded in the present moment.*

A good example of this was when Rick overheard a PE teacher coaching a netball team at half time. The team talk went something like this:

"Girls that was a great first half. We've got a decent lead and we're really playing well. But more importantly, just look at yourselves now (the girls actually turned to look at each other). You look like you're really enjoying the game. It's the first time, this season, I've seen you smiling and encouraging each other. That move towards the end of the first half when Tanya scored a goal was brilliant. All of you made at least one great pass. Just close your eyes and replay it in your mind (most of the team did actually close their eyes!). Let's go out for the second half, keep enjoying ourselves and move the ball around the same way."

The PE teacher was getting her players to catch the moment. She was highlighting the sense of achievement and enjoyment the team was having *at the time they were having it*.

We can all do this with children. Whenever we're having a positive time we can draw attention to the aspects that help build a child's confidence and self-esteem. The PE teacher did exactly this - she highlighted the positive atmosphere and team spirit and also drew attention to a good play when the team scored a goal.

Our warm-up activity of reflective listening can be used to reinforce catch the moment "What was the key skill when you scored that goal?" "How can you use that skill again in the second half?" We could also encourage the goal scorer to utilise another warm-up activity by adding the goal to her positive list.

Wendy is a great exponent of catching the moment. She never misses the opportunity to praise a child when they have done something positive. "Well done" is not enough to catch the moment, particularly for younger children who are not always sure what they've done well. Young children need specific clues that identify exactly what aspects of their behaviour we are highlighting, e.g. "Good listening. You really remembered the story well. Your concentration was great."

Catching the moment is about more than positive reinforcement. It's about making sure the positive aspect of a DVD is highlighted when it's recorded in a child's mind. Many of these moments simply fade away if they're not captured.

Anticipation.
Anticipation is another jogging exercise that builds on the idea of catching the moment but anticipation extends the thought from the present into the immediate future. Anticipating an enjoyable activity can be one of life's great pleasures and it also has the potential to create a positive self-fulfilling prophecy. If we can imagine ourselves having a good time we are actually more likely to have a good time. This encourages a more optimistic orientation, a view

that is supported by the research we mentioned on optimism and pessimism in Chapter 3.

Rick recalls a lovely summer day when he captured a moment with his children in the morning and then developed it into anticipation of the afternoon. It was a Saturday morning in June and the sun was shining brightly as he took the children shopping to the supermarket. In the afternoon it was England's first match in the Football World Cup against Paraguay. Rick and the children had been invited to his friend Ivan's home for a barbecue before watching the game on TV later in the afternoon. Ivan had also arranged a bouncy castle in the garden for the children to play on.

As they walked across the crowded supermarket car park Rick noticed how many of the cars were flying England flags, which fluttered brightly in the warm breeze. Rick stopped to enthuse about this wonderful sight to the children. The two boys, Sam and Jack, were enthralled to the degree that Sam took a picture on his camera phone. Rick's daughter, Martha, the youngest child, was smaller than the boys and hadn't been able to see the panoramic view because she was too small. Rick lifted her up and she was also amazed at the sight of literally dozens of cars flying the flag.

Having caught the moment, Rick then introduced the element of anticipation. As the children were watching the flags, Rick continued to enthuse about what a great sight this was and how much they would all enjoy the match, the barbecue and the bouncy castle in the afternoon. He then asked the children about their favourite barbecue food and what they were looking forward to doing at Ivan's house. Long after the World Cup was over, whenever they saw a car flying an England flag the children would often mention the day of the Paraguay match whilst replaying the DVD in their minds.

Again, you can see from this example how the warm-up activity of reflective listening can be used to reinforce anticipation. If the occasion is a real highlight for the child it can also be added to the positive list.

Creating Memories.
The next variation of jogging is creating a memory. As we mentioned earlier, Rick used to facilitate in-service training workshops for teachers in the USA on behalf of a friend of his, Gary Russell. After one session, Gary and Rick were having a beer together whilst reviewing the day's workshop and planning the next day's facilitation. Gary suddenly noticed the time and began to get up to go. He apologised for having to leave Rick to finish the planning for the next day's session but said he was off to "create a memory." On being quizzed as to what he meant, Gary explained that on most weekdays he had to work late and was often away from home travelling to other cities in the USA. However, in the football season, he always made a point of getting back in time to watch the Monday night football game with his young son, Chris. Gary would leave work early and stop off to buy pizza on the way home, which ensured that Monday night was a ritual that Chris always looked forward to. As Gary pointed out, he was consciously trying to make sure that Chris always remembered how important he was to his Dad by creating the memory of pizza and football on a Monday night.

Years later, Gary went on to write a very interesting book about how to find the elusive work/life balance called 'Big Rocks' (1).

Creating memories is about repeating a pleasant activity over a period of time. It involves planning ahead to deliberately select a positive experience which is grooved into the child's memory. Creating memories is about repetition and habit although some minor variation is a good idea – changing the toppings on the pizza, or even deciding to have a Chinese take-away might be a nice variation! Catching the moment and anticipation can be used to enhance and strengthen the memory, which is then filed as a DVD in the mind's library and can be replayed to help reinforce a child's self-confidence and esteem when times get tough.

Our jogging exercises are intended to focus children's consciousness on the positive things that are going on in their world. The focus with catching the moment is on the present; the exercise with anticipation focuses on the immediate future; and by creating memories the focus moves to the medium term future. The next set of mental training activities needs to be practised over a longer time period so that they can become lessons for life. These are our long steady runs.

Summary of Chapter 9
Jogging.

Catch the Moment
This activity is designed to encourage children to notice the good things in their lives by providing a commentary to the DVD *as it's being recorded in the present moment.* Catching the moment is about more than simply catching children being good. It's about making sure the positive aspect of a DVD is highlighted when it's recorded in a child's mind. Many of these moments simply fade away if they're not captured.

Anticipation
This is an exercise that builds on the idea of catching the moment but also extends it into the immediate future. Anticipating an enjoyable activity is not just a fun activity, it also has the potential to create a positive self-fulfilling prophecy. If we can imagine ourselves having a good time we are actually more likely to have a good time. This encourages a more optimistic view of the world.

Creating memories
Creating memories is about repeating a pleasant activity over a period of time. It involves planning ahead to deliberately select a positive experience which is then grooved into the child's memory. Creating memories is about repetition and habit, although some minor variation is a good idea. Catching the moment and anticipation can be used to enhance and strengthen the memory, which is then filed as a DVD in the mind's library and can be replayed to help reinforce a child's self-confidence and esteem when times get tough.

Chapter 10
Long Steady Runs.

The very nature of these activities means that they will take more time to conclude, unlike most of our jogging exercises, which are more spontaneous and relate to single events (although creating memories may involve multiple events). In contrast to jogging, long steady runs usually have an element of continuity about them.

Diary Keeping.
The first of our long steady runs is diary keeping. It's a technique that Rick uses with adults who are suffering from psychological distress but it can easily be utilised with children. Diaries are a useful form of recording children's thoughts whether it's for general improvement of confidence and self-esteem or where there is a more specific deep seated problem which is causing a child to suffer from anxiety or depression.

Diary keeping builds on some of the previous exercises, and when reviewing the diary with the child it opens up lots of opportunities for using reflective listening. Recording a diary is an exercise best done at the end of the day on a regular basis in order to make the child's positive thinking more systematic – practice makes permanent.

The instructions for keeping the diary are quite simple. At the end of every day the child needs to write down a few sentences to describe what happened over the course of the day. Then they are asked to rate the day in terms of how it felt:

1 = It was a terrible day to 10 = It was a fantastic day.

If the score for the day is on the low side, the child is encouraged to read the list of thinking errors to see if they are making any negative assumptions about the day which, if successfully challenged, will prove to be false. As a result of the successful challenges the scores often improve.

Recording the thoughts and feelings on the day that they occur is a powerful way of helping children to do a number of things. It allows them to make comparisons between days and with our help they can also track patterns to see whether there are certain triggers that cause them to score certain days higher or lower than others. Most importantly though, it gives them a chance to challenge their thinking errors as they occur.

If the scores are consistently low this may be due to certain thinking errors locking the filter in place so that the positive memories of the day are stuck in the subconscious mind.

The following example is taken from 'The Promised Land' and it refers to a young man called Martin who was suffering from depression and was working with Rick. This example shows how effective Martin's thinking errors were at locking the filter in place. The thinking error he was making on this particular day for his diary entry was to disqualify a positive experience.

Martin came from a large family with seven brothers and sisters. He was currently experiencing a number of life events: the premature death of one of his brothers; a terminally ill sister; the recent break up with his girlfriend; and he had also been involved in a car crash, which had knocked his confidence.

At one of his counselling sessions with Rick, Martin was recounting a particularly low scoring day, which on his scale of 1 – 10, he had rated 2. He described how stressed he'd felt at work because he was focussed on the support he had to give his terminally ill sister and the fact that he didn't want to drive to a sales meeting for fear of crashing the car. He also commented on the sadness he felt over the fact that he had no emotional support in dealing with these issues. As soon as he got home he had a difficult phone call from his deceased brother's partner about some legal issues that had arisen because his brother had died without making a will.

Martin felt thoroughly depressed and his rating of 2 for this particular day reflected this. Rick noticed that Martin hadn't commented in his diary on what he'd done that evening. When Rick asked him what he'd done that evening, Martin closed his eyes and started to retrieve the DVD memory. After he'd located the memory in his library Martin nodded his head and then smiled. "Actually I went to choir practice that evening"- Martin sang in a gospel choir at his local church. He then recounted his attendance at choir practice. He had enjoyed the singing and the camaraderie of going for a drink and a meal afterwards with some of his friends. Rick asked him why he hadn't written about this in his diary. Martin's reply was "Well, it doesn't really count."

On further gentle probing it appeared that Martin felt it was somehow wrong to acknowledge anything positive in his life because he had to focus on the more pressing negative events he was dealing with. (This often applies to children dealing with stressful life events). Finally Rick asked Martin "Taking into account the choir practice, how would you rate the day retrospectively?" Martin thought for a while and eventually said "Well, taking the evening into account as well, the day as a whole would have rated at least a five."

Whilst this example focuses on a young man it could easily refer to a child. The principles are exactly the same. Wendy worked with a Year 6 child, Maya, who was having tearful moments during the day. Maya's teacher commented that Maya was "always bursting into tears." Wendy and Maya started a 'feelings diary' and found that in reality Maya didn't cry as much as her teacher believed – the teacher was making a thinking error. Wendy and Maya then made a 'feelings graph' showing how many tearful moments there were at the moment and how Maya would like to reduce these. Diary keeping is an excellent way to practice challenging the thinking errors. To paraphrase Shakespeare, 'no day is a bad day but thinking makes it so'. Even on our most difficult days good things happen but they just get filtered out. By helping children to challenge the thinking errors and re-set the filter the good things are noticed. When we notice the good things this improves the way we feel about the day.

Friendships.

Our second long steady run is to help children to develop friendships. Having friends is potentially one of the greatest resources we can have in helping us to get through life's difficulties. In a recent study by Fairweather et al (1) 522 people aged between 20 – 44 from a massive community survey admitted they had thought about taking their own life in the last year. Slightly less than 10% of these people had also reported actually making an attempt to commit suicide. The individuals who had attempted suicide were more likely to have serious ill health, to be unemployed and to have poor relationships with friends and family.

Being lonely and having few people with whom we can share both life's triumphs and troubles seriously impacts on our psychological well being. In Chapter 1 we mentioned the research in the BBC documentary, 'The Happiness Formula', which concluded that friendship had a greater impact on people's happiness than wealth.

It is vitally important to try to help children to develop friendships with their peers. Many of us assume that making friends 'just happens' but if we can help children to think about the concept of friendship and to understand the effort that needs to go into making and keeping friends, we will be helping them to develop a valuable life skill. Discussing this concept with children and using reflective listening to encourage them to think more deeply about this is a great exercise.

Broadly speaking, we are initially attracted by similarity: the more we have in common with someone, at least in the early stages of a relationship, then the more likely we are to get on with that person. So it's really useful to encourage children to interact with peers who have similar backgrounds and interests, or who are in similar situations. Teachers and childminders can help facilitate this by trying to integrate children who seem to have few friends by consciously putting them into workgroups where they can mix with other children with whom they may have something in common. There are many ways that schools help in promoting awareness of friendship. Exercises and topics such as: defining what a friend is;

creating friendship recipes which include all the 'ingredients' of friendship; designing a friendship wheel, which involves making and sharing friendship bracelets; and compiling a list of friendly deeds. Schools also encourage peer support by giving older children responsibility for identifying children who appear to be lonely or upset in the playground.

Wendy also looks for opportunities for children to make friends in the wider community. There can be great benefits from a child befriending an older person.

It's also important for parents to play their part in cultivating their children's friendships, not just with peers but also making friends with other family members, such as brothers and sisters or cousins. It's easy to assume that children will have a good relationship with their siblings but, unless it's encouraged when they are young, it may not happen. When children create a positive list, friends and family usually feature on the list and it's important to reinforce the benefits of friendship through the use of reflective listening.

Uniqueness.
Building an awareness of a child's uniqueness is another long steady run that has the potential to hugely increase their self-esteem. In Wendy's experience children aged between seven to eleven often don't want to be different. However, they later come to equate uniqueness with being 'special'. Understanding our uniqueness becomes more important in life as we get older. Higher levels of self-awareness mean we are able to make the best use of our individual ability later in life. Being self-aware also helps us to avoid, or try to modify, situations that we are not well suited for. Above all, a sense of uniqueness teaches children that it's not simply 'okay' to be different, it can actually be a great benefit. Lots of situations in life involve working as part of a team and having different skills within a team is a great advantage.

In Chapter 4 we spent some time looking at the 'Human Factors Model' which accounts for who we grow up to be and why we fit certain situations well and others less well. The model describes how we inherit some traits through the effects of nature (the result of the genes we inherit) and how other traits are inherited through the effects of nurture (the environment we are brought up in, and the situations we experience). Because of the effects of nature even young children may not be able to change some of their traits much, despite the later influence of nurture. So, helping children to become more self-aware and to celebrate their uniqueness from a relatively early age can help to build their long-term self-esteem.

One way that Wendy helps to reinforce children's sense of uniqueness is to fingerprint the children she spends time working one-to-one with. She then reinforces the fact that they are different and special. Fingerprints also demonstrate that some things don't change over time, we will always be uniquely different – just like everyone else!

Because we are talking about trying to change children's thinking patterns it's important to remember that this isn't about changing who the child is as a person. In fact, to a large degree, it's the opposite: it's about helping the child to accept who they are, whilst trying to change their perception of difficult situations so that they can fashion the situation to suit themselves. Psychologically healthy individuals are able to change their perception of their ability to handle their external world. Quite often the changes required are relatively minor.

Rick's elder son, Sam, had quite a high pitched voice when he was young. At the age of nine he moved to a middle school which was quite a step up from the small village primary school he had previously attended. The middle school had over 400 children, aged from nine to thirteen. Sam was one of the youngest kids in his year and also one of the smallest. In a short space of time he was teased by the other children because of his high pitched voice and was dubbed 'squeaky'. Initially he was very upset about this.

However, without any prompting, he changed his perception of the teasing. Rather than focus on 'squeaky' as a description of his voice he used the name 'Squeaky' as a nickname, which eventually became a positive aspect of his identity. Like many of his friends he was a keen football fan and supported his local team, Wolverhampton Wanderers. When he was given a replica Wolves shirt for his birthday he asked if he could have his nickname Squeaky emblazoned on the back of the shirt. He adopted a more hip version 'Squeakachino' as his e-mail address. Often Rick and his children would be walking through the village and a group of kids, many of them older than Sam, would cycle by and shout "Hiya Squeak!" in Sam's direction at which Sam would grin and shout "Hiya" back. Perhaps the ultimate proof of having turned a negative into a positive was when Rick watched him play football for his school team a couple of years later. As Rick was shouting encouragement to him, Sam came over to the touchline in a break in play and asked Rick not to call him Sam but to call him Squeak, which was how his team-mates referred to him.

Sam couldn't control the fact that other children at the school initially used the word 'squeaky' to ridicule a physical trait. However, he was able to control his perception of the adjective. He viewed it as a positive aspect of his identity - it set him apart from his fellow students. There were plenty of other children called Sam in his school – there was only one Squeaky.

Using a modified version of the positive list combined with reflective listening can also play a part in building a sense of uniqueness. Getting children to list what it is they like about themselves and what their friends and family see as their best qualities and attributes can be very effective. Asking a child to get some feedback from friends and family about what it is that makes them unique can also be a very self-affirming exercise. These techniques can also help to overlap with the concept of friendship.

When children get their school reports, parents should consider spending more time enthusing about what their children have a real talent for and less time berating them for being poor at certain subjects or activities. This is another element of uniqueness. We're not condoning lack of effort or laziness on the part of children who just can't be bothered. There are, however, relatively few children who are talented all-rounders, so it makes sense to enthuse about each child's best subjects.

As Wendy points out, often a child may have a talent in a non-academic area and as long as they are trying hard to get the basic educational requirements, the more we can enthuse about what they have a talent for then the more this builds their confidence and self-esteem. Educating children involves more than simply instilling academic knowledge. A school report that provides a broader picture of the child contains good opportunities for building a child's self-esteem. True self-confidence is about being comfortable with the fact that you're not good at certain activities because you know that you have a real talent for other things. It helps to use the reflective listening technique to engage with children about their school report. The use of open questions helps both children and parents to understand what the report tells us about each child as an individual.

As we mentioned earlier, the long steady runs can involve learning lessons for life. Using a daily diary to help children's reflections, learning how to make and keep friends, and developing children's levels of self-awareness so that they understand what makes them unique all fall into this category. Sometimes in life, however, we need more short-term and intense exercises to deal with specific life events and these form the short sprints of our training programme.

Summary of Chapter 10
Long Steady Runs.

Diary Keeping.
As a child becomes more aware of how their filter is working, keeping a diary enables them to raise their levels of consciousness about what type of thoughts are being registered in their conscious mind. Using the diary helps to challenge the thinking errors. Asking children to rate their day from 1 – 10 encourages them to challenge the validity of low scores. They can critically assess whether low scores reflect the thinking errors which have locked the negative filter in place and caused the positive aspects that occurred during the day to remain unnoticed. This is a powerful exercise for mental fitness training, especially when combined with reflective listening.

Friendships.
Developing friendships is potentially one of the greatest resources we can have in helping us to get through life's difficulties. Research links lack of friends to poor psychological well being. If we can help children to think about the concept of friendship and to understand the effort that needs to go into making and keeping friends, we will be helping them to develop a valuable life skill. Discussing this concept with children and using reflective listening to encourage them to think more deeply about this is a great exercise.

Whilst it's important to develop friendships with peer groups, we shouldn't ignore the opportunities for children to make friends with people in the wider community, such as older people. There are also opportunities to develop strong 'friendships' with family members, especially siblings and cousins. It's important not to assume that these relationships will just develop into friendships without some conscious effort on the part of parents.

Uniqueness.
Building an awareness of a child's uniqueness is important in helping to develop their self-esteem. Younger children may not

want to be seen as different, however it becomes more important as children get older. Higher levels of self-awareness mean we are able to make best use of our uniqueness later in life. Chapter 4 described the 'Human Factors Model', which accounts for how we inherit our traits through both nature and nurture. Even young children may not be able to change some of their traits because they have inherited them through their genes. The concept of uniqueness recognises that we are only trying to change children's thinking patterns with regard to themselves. We are not trying to fundamentally change the child as a person. In fact, to a large degree, it's the opposite: it's about helping the child to celebrate their uniqueness.

CHAPTER 11
SHORT SPRINTS.

Sometimes children go through relatively short, but more painful experiences, where they need specific exercises that are designed to deal with this type of experience. Whilst some of the previous exercises can be adapted to help with negative life events, our sprinting exercises can be particularly effective in dealing with these.

Well Formed Outcomes.
In specific circumstances we may need a really clear plan of action to help a child re-build their confidence and esteem. The first sprint exercise focuses on the importance of getting clarity about what the child wants to achieve. Richard Bandler and John Grinder (1) who devised the theory of neurolinguistic programming (NLP), noticed in their research on successful therapists that the therapists who were most effective asked their clients to define precisely what it was that they wanted to achieve from the therapy – a well formed outcome. We can adapt this technique to help children who are struggling with life events.

By getting children to define clearly the outcome they want, two things happen. First it becomes possible to measure the progress they are making towards improving their confidence and esteem. The clarity helps to do this – only by knowing the destination of the journey is it possible to estimate how far along the road the child is. Second, being able to visualise what the destination looks like can be a powerful motivator in terms of helping children through the difficult parts of the journey. By getting children to write down their well formed outcomes we are able to keep a written record, which can be used to assess their progress towards the outcomes. The outcomes can also form the basis of some useful dialogue when combined with reflective listening.

There are seven questions that help to define more precisely what each child's outcomes might be:

1. "What outcomes do you want to achieve from this?"

This is a very broad question but the greater the clarity the better. Some of the subsequent questions help to achieve greater clarity. There are no right or wrong answers to this question. However, it's worth remembering that if you want to be able to measure your progress towards the outcome, the more specific the outcome is then the easier it is to see how much progress you're making towards it.

2. "Where, when and with who do you want to achieve your outcomes?"

This helps to narrow down the focus. Sometimes children have a specific problem related to their schoolwork, or it might be a confidence problem dealing with a specific group of people. Alternatively, it could be a problem relating to a relationship that is troubling the child. Putting a realistic time frame on achieving the outcome is important in helping to chart the progress made. It's easy to get disheartened if we set an unrealistically short timeframe. Often children have been struggling for many months, or even years, with their negative perception of the world. It's unrealistic to think that this perception might be turned around in just a couple of weeks.

3. "What will it look, sound and feel like when I've achieved my outcomes?"

Imagining a positive future can be very important in helping to motivate a child when the effort seems too much. Having an attractive picture of what the future might hold if their outcomes are achieved spurs most children on. Some children also benefit from thinking about what might happen if they *don't* manage to achieve their outcomes. A dark and miserable picture of a future with unachieved outcomes can be a sobering thought.

4. "Are you in control of the changes necessary to help you achieve your outcomes?"
This is potentially a difficult question, but it throws some light on what a child can and can't control. It emphasises the balance between what the child needs to accept and what they are able to change. The consequence of understanding this balance helps them to understand where they should channel their energies.

5. "Will I lose anything if I succeed in achieving my outcomes?"
There are often potential losses when children achieve their outcomes. For example, if a child has been using drugs but wants to stop, saying 'no' to the pressure of being offered drugs may mean losing a group of friends. Loss is a difficult concept because it has to be weighed against the potential gains, hence the next question.

6. "Is the outcome worth the effort?"
If the child feels the outcome isn't worth the effort we need to ask the child some more questions. Are they really clear about the potential positive benefits of making the changes in their thinking? Do they understand the potential negative long-term consequences of not changing their thinking? If, on the other hand, the answer to this question is an unequivocal 'yes' and the outcome is worth the effort then it's important to reiterate that they don't cheat on how much honest effort they put into changing their thinking.

7. "What will all the positive consequences be of achieving my outcomes?"
Get the child to list as many benefits that will emanate from being able to re-set their filter to notice all the positive things about them and their life. This may overlap with some of the other questions but that's a good thing – hopefully it reaffirms what they already know, that the outcome will be worth the effort.

There are no right or wrong answers in well formed outcomes, they simply offer an opportunity to help the child to explore their own thinking. By using reflective listening when they share their outcomes we can help children to get greater levels of clarity. It may not be appropriate to use well formed outcomes for every child who has a general problem with low levels of confidence. However, where it is appropriate, this short sprint can be used early on in the process and then supplemented by using some of the other training techniques described earlier.

Decision making.

As we mentioned in Chapter 6, it's really important to feel that we have some control over our lives. Our next sprint exercise is about helping children to feel a greater sense of control through being more actively involved in decision making. The research by Fairweather et al (2) on suicide noted that for men in particular, not feeling in control of the forces affecting their lives was linked to increased likelihood of attempting suicide. Children who are experiencing negative life events often feel they have little control over their lives. The lack of control may be real - as in a situation where a child's parents are in the process of divorcing, or it may be a *perceived* lack of control. If it's perceived the child may have more control over the outcome than they believe.

Where the lack of control is real there may not be much the child can do to affect the situation. The key in these situations is to help the child talk through their problems by using reflective listening, but then to try to encourage them to let go of the problem and channel their energies into something they can control. In these cases Wendy tries to enhance the child's ability to take decisions in lots of unrelated situations. A ten-year-old lad Wendy worked with, called Donovan, had a variety of different carers looking after him because of a very unstable situation with his parents. As a result of this, Donovan felt that he had no control or consistency in his life. Wendy negotiated, with the Headteacher to purchase a fish tank, complete with fish. It was agreed that Donovan would be responsible for feeding the fish, and with the caretaker's guidance, Donovan would help to clean it out. This gave Donovan a sense of control, routine and stability that was missing in an otherwise fragmented life.

Where the lack of control is *perceived* it's important to provide the child with as much information as possible to increase the number of options available and to help the child think through the options by using reflective listening. For example a child may not be able to control whether their parents divorce, but they may be able to influence where they live, who they live with, what school they want to attend, how they want to maintain relationships with both parents. The greater a child's circle of influence then the more likely they are to be able to help control the outcome.

Stephen Covey, in his book 'The Seven Habits of Highly Effective People' (3) suggests that we have a circle of influence and a circle of concern. Covey argues that proactive people focus their efforts on their circle of influence where they work on the things they can do something about. The nature of their energy is positive, enlarging and magnifying. Reactive people, however, concentrate on the circle of concern. Their focus is on the weakness of other people and the circumstances over which they have no control. As a result, they end up blaming or accusing other people, and their own feelings of victimisation are increased. The more we help children to work on their circle of influence the more their confidence and esteem will benefit.

A useful example of this was a Sunday football match that Rick was watching between two teams of 13-year-old lads. Two of the parents from one team became incensed at some of the referee's decisions. In particular, they felt that the referee was being too lenient with some very physical play by the opposing team, including one robust challenge that had injured one of their players. The two parents protested loudly to the referee from the side of the pitch and made a number of remarks commenting on how unfair he was being. Shortly after this the referee blew his whistle for half time.

The two parents walked across to where the young coach of their team was giving his half time talk. One of the parents again bemoaned how unfair the referee had been with his decisions. The coach acknowledged this, but immediately told his players that they had no control over the referee and that they should channel their efforts into two things. The first thing was to make sure they chased every ball without giving up, and to encourage each other every time one of them did something well. The second thing was to recognise that despite some of the foul play from the opposition, they should feel proud that they had continued to compete fairly without resorting to retaliation. Focusing on the circle of concern i.e. the poor standard of refereeing would lead only to blame, accusations and a feeling of victimisation. Focusing on the circle of influence i.e. chasing every ball, encouraging each other and feeling proud about not retaliating would lead to greater feelings of confidence and self-esteem.

Visualisation.

As we suggested in Chapter 10, the long steady runs are a good way of gradually adjusting the filter. However, in some cases children have very powerful sad and painful DVD memories that have the potential to dominate their thinking. In these circumstances a child's anxieties and fears can simply overtake their mind to the extent that they find it difficult to concentrate on the exercises described previously. In dealing with this type of situation we may need a different sprinting technique - visualisation.

Visualisation involves helping children to revisit memories from the past or to imagine situations in the future. Sometimes it's necessary to revisit painful past memories with a view to 'diluting' them so that they have less power to negatively affect a child. Visualisation can also be used to help children focus on past positive experiences in order to help build a child's belief that they are a successful person. Another application for visualisation is to help a child to imagine how it would look, sound and feel to be successful at some future event.

As we mentioned earlier, one of the ways children try to cope with very powerful negative memories is to place them in a box on a shelf at the back of the mind's library with a heavy weight on the box to make the sure the lid doesn't fly off. The problem with this approach is that the child is acutely aware of the presence of this box in the back of the library. Even if they don't open the box, they still know it's there with all the painful memories stowed inside.

In an ideal world, in order to exorcise the negative feelings of these painful memories we need to help children gradually open the box. Slowly confronting the anger, fear, sadness and sorrow, with the help of a trained counsellor is probably the most effective way to reduce the power of these DVDs to hurt the child. After a time the child learns to forgive all the parties involved in these painful events – including themselves. Visualisation can be used effectively to help this process.

It's not the aim of this book to turn everyone who reads it into a counsellor, but there are valid reasons for including visualisation as a sprint exercise. First, it's not a particularly complex technique. Visualisation has proved itself in a variety of disciplines outside the clinical field, most notably with sports psychology. For many years Rick worked for the National Coaching Foundation and delivered training programmes designed to equip sports coaches with the fundamental techniques for visualisation. The applications of visualisation for enhancing positive past experiences and imagining successful future experiences are not contentious. Second, visualisation is a very useful training technique for dealing with nervousness and anxiety. It works well as a relaxation technique and many parents will have unwittingly used a form of visualisation in, for example, helping anxious children who can't sleep.

Many people would not feel comfortable using the technique to dilute powerful painful memories, and this may be best left to a trained counsellor. However, we've included the following example because it will demonstrate how the technique works with both diluting powerful negative past memories and enhancing positive past memories.

Rick once worked with a boy of eight, called Vinny, who had become very anxious that a stranger would kidnap him, an idea that had been sewn in his mind by the kidnap and subsequent murder of a young girl. Although the kidnapping had occurred over a hundred miles from where Vinny lived, the event, not surprisingly, got massive media coverage. The journalists who reported on this story also rehashed previous similar events from the last 20 years, which made the problem of kidnapping seem far more common than it actually is.

Vinny was a happy child most of the time but his mother had noticed an increasing reluctance for him to go anywhere on his own. Vinny lived in a small village and his grandparents lived literally 100 metres along the street next to a newsagent. Prior to the kidnap Vinny would happily pop to the shop for his mum or walk down the road to visit his grandparents. After the kidnap he was very anxious about doing this and the problem got progressively worse. When his mum visited petrol stations with Vinny and his younger sister in the car, Vinny would refuse to wait in the car whilst his mum went to pay at the kiosk. He feared that a stranger would approach the car and kidnap him.

It got to the stage that the anxiety of being kidnapped preyed on Vinny's mind so much that he was finding any excuse to stay in the house rather than go out to play with friends or take part in organised activities. Then Vinny started to get occasional nightmares in which he saw himself being kidnapped by a man with a beard. Vinny's mum became increasingly worried about him and decided to seek Rick's help.

After Rick listened to Vinny and his mum talking about Vinny's life in general and how he had become anxious about being kidnapped Rick became aware of two factors. The first factor was that Vinny's mum and dad were recently divorced and although it had been a very civilised divorce with both parties remaining friendly it played on Vinny's mind. The second factor was that Vinny's mum seemed to be quite an anxious woman herself, some of her own statements about the kidnapping suggested quite a high degree of threat sensitivity. Both these factors indicated that Vinny may already have had his filters set to notice negative DVDs. Rick explained the theory of the mind as a DVD library and how Vinny's filter appeared to be set to notice all the negative events in his life. Vinny and his mum agreed that this seemed to be exactly what was happening.

Rick listened to Vinny describe the nightmares he was experiencing and it became evident that the man in the nightmares looked like the photofit picture that the police had issued with regard to the suspect. Rick then talked to Vinny about the things that made him feel very positive and asked him to make a positive list for his next session. Rick also asked Vinny, with the help of his mum, to complete his well formed outcomes which seemed appropriate in this case.

At the next session Rick used reflective listening as Vinny went through both his outcomes and his positive list. Rick was pleased to hear that Vinny had enjoyed compiling his list and that when he read it out to his mum he felt very positive about himself. Rick then asked Vinny about the nightmares. Vinny looked visibly upset and said that he was still getting them. As he described the nightmares his mum started to become tearful. His mum mentioned that she had tried to challenge some of the thinking errors that Vinny was making about kidnapping. However, Vinny became so panicky when certain cues reminded him of the kidnap incident that he was unable to think rationally about challenging any of his thinking errors. When his mum was filling up with petrol, for example, he knew his mum was only a few metres away but his anxiety simply overwhelmed him.

Rick then asked Vinny which of the things on his list made him feel the most positive about himself. Vinny looked down his list and picked out the time when he had been to a soccer coaching course and at the end of the week he had won a penalty shootout competition and been given a silver coloured medal.

To win the medal Vinny competed with a group of over 30 children who each took penalty kicks against a peer who was the goalkeeper. It was a 'sudden death' competition - each time a player missed they were eliminated from the competition. All the players who scored carried on to the next round. After five rounds there were only three players left who had scored every penalty so far. One of them was Vinny. In round six, the other players took their penalties first. One lad blasted his shot over the bar and the second boy had his spot kick saved by the goalkeeper. All the pressure was on Vinny to score. As Vinny recalled this DVD memory he remembered how calm and focused he felt when he placed the ball down. He also remembered the noise all the kids were making, some cheering him on, others willing him to miss. He described running up to the ball and striking it cleanly with his right foot and watching it hit the back of the net low down in the right corner of the goal. As Vinny described it to Rick, Rick noticed the change in the boy. Confidence and esteem seemed to flow through him as he recalled his winning performance.

With the agreement of both Vinny and his mum, Rick suggested that they try a visualisation exercise the following week. It would involve revisiting the nightmare DVD in detail whilst Vinny was awake, but with his eyes closed. However, with Rick's help Vinny would change some of the detail in this DVD. Then Rick would ask Vinny to recall the penalty shoot out DVD in as much vivid detail as possible. Rick asked Vinny to prepare some notes recalling everything about the penalty shootout using all his senses - the sights, the sounds and the feelings it evoked.

At the next session Rick used the following visualisation technique for helping to dilute the power of the nightmare. In order to utilise this technique Rick needed two DVD memories: the negative one that was causing the problem i.e. Vinny's nightmare; and a very positive unrelated DVD memory i.e. the penalty shootout. (The positive memory should preferably be one in which the child feels empowered, in control and confident).

The technique Rick used involves taking the negative memory and deliberately changing the modalities in the memory. We literally change what we see, hear and feel in the memory as if it were a DVD being shown on a TV screen. In this way, the power of the negative memory is diluted. We can then link the negative memory to the positive memory, which we enhance by changing the modalities to make the positive memory even more vibrant and exciting. This has the effect of making the negative memory the cue for triggering the positive memory. In other words, we set up a chain – when thoughts of the kidnapping or the nightmare came into Vinny's head this became the cue for thinking about the penalty shootout. Interestingly, if you always maintain the order of DVDs it seems that they only work in one direction – thoughts of the penalty shootout shouldn't cue the kidnap.

The following narrative explains how the technique works in general. The object is to get the child to view first the negative DVD, but we want them to disassociate with it i.e. they are not part of the DVD, they are merely a viewer watching themselves. We encourage them to verbalise what they can see and hear but then we encourage the child to take control of the DVD by imagining they have a very special remote control so they can change what happens in the DVD thereby evoking less painful emotions. We then help the child to 'dilute' the DVD and then finally the child will turn off the DVD.

We then start to play the child's positive DVD. The child can use their special remote control to enhance this DVD memory and we introduce the other senses that allow the child to associate with this memory i.e. feelings (both emotional and kinaesthetic), smell and taste if appropriate.

The narrative for this technique might be as follows:

➢ Take the negative DVD and begin to watch it with your eyes closed, but imagine that you are watching the DVD on a TV screen for which you have a very special remote control.
➢ Remember you are watching yourself on the DVD. You are not part of the DVD action (disassociation).
➢ As you are watching the DVD tell me what you can see. What do all the characters look like? What expressions are on their faces? Describe what colours you can see in the DVD.
➢ Now use the remote control to turn the colours to black and white so that it looks like an old film.
➢ Now tell me what sounds you can hear. What are people saying? Describe their voices.

> ➤ Press some of the buttons on the remote control so that you can alter the way people are talking. Make them high pitched and funny or very low and slow.
> ➤ Now use the remote control to turn the sound all the way down until it has become a silent movie and watch the people in the DVD saying things without any sounds coming out of their mouths.
> ➤ Press another button on your remote control. This button turns the DVD into slow motion so all the characters look quite surreal in their movements.
> ➤ Now press another button and freeze the frame. In the picture you've frozen, the main perpetrator of the negative behaviour is caught mid sentence with their mouth open and their eyes shut. They look very silly.
> ➤ Press the contrast button on the remote control so that the quality of the picture becomes very poor and the screen appears to have a snowstorm effect. Notice how the clarity of the images become gradually less and less distinct.
> ➤ Finally, press another button on the remote control that shrinks the picture down to a white dot in the centre of the screen.
> ➤ Using your remote control like the mouse from a computer, click and drag this dot to one corner of the screen, for example, top left.

We now need to utilise the positive DVD.

> ➤ Now press another button on the remote control.
> ➤ This time the screen is filled by a very positive DVD. You can watch the DVD but this time you are also part of the action (association).
> ➤ Describe what you see happening in the DVD. Tell me what happens next. What colours can you see in this DVD?
> ➤ Press a button on your remote control to adjust the colour to make them as bright and vivid as possible.
> ➤ Tell me what you see yourself doing. Describe how that feels. Adjust the picture to make it as clear and sharp as possible so that you can see all the little details in the picture.

> Tell me what you can hear. Describe what people are saying and how they are saying it. Describe their voices. Use the remote control to tune the sound in so that it's wonderfully clear without being loud. Imagine the sound is in stereo. Imagine there is a favourite musical soundtrack accompanying the images.

> Tell me what the temperature feels like. Describe the atmosphere. When you're touching things in the DVD, describe how they feel.

> Finally, at the most positive point in the film, freeze the frame and admire the picture you've just created in wonderful technicolour and listen to the beautiful soundtrack.

> Now, using the remote control shrink this picture down to a dot in the centre of the screen. Click and drag the dot to the opposite corner of the screen to the first dot, for example, bottom right.

> Now click and drag the 'negative' dot from the top left of the screen and bring it to the centre of the screen, open up the negative dot and run the DVD picture.

Ideally, we would now repeat the process of showing the negative DVD followed by the positive DVD twice more, *always* finishing with the positive DVD.

By watching the child's reactions as they describe each DVD we can focus on particularly significant images. With the negative images we can work hard to change them. For example, Vinny was particularly troubled by the man's face in his nightmare DVD so Rick got him to change his DVD so that the man wore a clown's red nose, which made Vinny laugh out loud. With the positive DVD, enhance anything that seems to evoke a particularly positive reaction. Vinny was particularly delighted when he described the noise of the ball hitting the net and the backboard behind the goal (the coaching course was held in an indoor location). As he described scoring the goal with his eyes shut Rick noticed he clenched his fist and punched the air as the ball hit the net.

This technique attempts to do a number of things utilising some powerful elements of neurolinguistic programming - NLP (2). One of the main tenets of NLP suggests that we think by using our three most predominant senses - visual (pictures), auditory (sound) and kinaesthetic (feelings). By using these modalities we can dilute the negative DVDs and enhance the positive DVDs very effectively. Anthony Robbins (4) has written extensively in more depth how NLP techniques can be harnessed in this way.

At the next session Rick took the visualisation with Vinny a stage further. Rick introduced an 'anchor' for the positive DVD picture that Vinny described when he scored the goal. Anchors are words and gestures that sum up perfectly how the person feels at the culmination of the positive DVD. The gesture has to be something fairly unobtrusive but unique to the positive DVD rather than an everyday common gesture. The word or phrase should also capture the uniqueness of the moment. Vinny chose the word 'silver' which was the colour of his medal and his gesture was the clenched fist.

Each time we repeated the positive DVD at the point that Vinny described his winning penalty kick and froze the frame on the TV screen, Rick asked him to say the word silver in a confident voice and clench his fist tightly. Rick and Vinny were anchoring all the positive elements of the DVD to the word and the gesture so that Vinny could access the feelings without necessarily running the full DVD. As we mentioned earlier, on some occasions Vinny became so panicky when certain cues reminded him of the kidnap incident that he was unable to think rationally about challenging any of his thinking errors. However, if Vinny said the word 'silver' and clenched his fist he would hopefully cue the positive feelings, which had been anchored to these cues.

Vinny agreed that the next time he found himself feeling anxious he would try this out. His mum made a point of visiting the petrol station on the way home from our session and Vinny was successfully able to stay in the car without getting panicky by using his anchor.

Negative DVDs can sometimes pop into our heads for no apparent reason. They can be triggered by a cue such as something we see, hear, touch, smell or taste. Sometimes these triggers are so subtle that we may not even be aware of them at the time because they operate at a subconscious level. For example, Vinny might have found himself walking along the road and for no apparent reason a negative DVD might start to play about kidnaps, causing Vinny to feel very anxious. Something in Vinny's subconscious mind will have triggered this thought and because it's in his subconscious mind he won't even be aware of it. It could be that a similar car to the one used in the kidnap happened to drive by, or Vinny passed a man with a beard and without realising it the negative DVD started to play with the accompanying anxiety. (In Chapter 2 we mentioned the example of Emma and the sign for 'Millet's Farm Store' as an example of sub-conscious triggers).

So, whilst Vinny may not be able to prevent the negative memories from coming into his mind, by practising the technique of diluting the negative memory it strips the DVD of its power to cause him so much discomfort. Then, because we've used the negative DVD itself as the cue to trigger the positive DVD (by connecting the two closely together), hopefully the positive DVD will start to come into his mind. Finally, even if he's initially unable to get the positive DVD to play because he's feeling too panicky, if Vinny uses the anchor it should trigger the positive feelings to combat the panic, and the positive DVD should start playing. The more we get a child to practice this then the greater their ability to run the positive DVD effortlessly through 'firing' the anchor by using the word or phrase and the accompanying gesture.

In Vinny's example, the negative DVD of his nightmare was a combination of negative memories and imagined fears. It doesn't matter whether the negative DVD is real or imagined it still has the power to cause the cycle of self-doubt, lack of confidence and low self-esteem.

Visualisation can of course be used to simply enhance positive images of the past without the involvement of diluting a negative image. It can be used to help us relax and promote feelings of self-confidence and, by visualising future events, we increase the likelihood of positive self-fulfilling prophecies. If a child can imagine what a successful outcome will look, sound and feel like, we can help them to programme their mind so that their body actually delivers the successful outcome in real life.

The short sprints are the most intense part of our mental fitness-training programme. In the next chapter we'll be focusing on some exercises that are designed to help sustain the momentum a child will hopefully have already achieved by this stage in the programme. The activities in the next chapter are aimed at encouraging children to start thinking about the future – these are our warm-down exercises.

Summary of Chapter 11
Short Sprints.

Well Formed Outcomes.
When assisting children to deal with specific issues, clarity is very important to help them to overcome their psychological distress. By answering the seven questions to establish their well formed outcomes, children who are experiencing stress, anxiety or depression gain the clarity necessary to see what it is they want, and the changes that need to be made to get it.

Through combining this with reflective thinking and other exercises from the mental fitness-training programme, we can help children to identify the most pernicious thinking errors and then challenge these more effectively.

Decision Making.
As we mentioned earlier in Chapter 6 it's really important to feel that we have some control over our lives. Children experiencing life events often feel they have little control over their lives. This may be real, or it may be perceived.

In situations where the lack of control is *real* there may not be much the child can do. The key in these situations is to help the child talk through their problems by using reflective listening, but then to try to encourage them to let go of the problem and channel their energies into something they can control.

Where the lack of control is *perceived* it's important to provide the child with as much information as possible to increase the number of options available and to help the child think through these options by using reflective listening. In doing this we increase the child's ability to influence situations. The greater a child's sphere of influence then the more likely they are to be able to control the outcome.

Visualisation.

Using the power of the mind to help overcome painful negative memories and enhance positive memories is a very effective way of ensuring that the positive DVDs are the closest to hand in the child's mental DVD library. Visualisation is particularly effective when a negative DVD memory is so powerful that it hinders a child's ability to challenge the thinking errors.

Diluting the power of the negative DVD memory allows the child to start challenging the thinking errors. Linking the negative memory to a positive DVD memory makes the negative memory a cue that triggers the positive memory. Using a phrase and gesture to anchor the positive DVD memory allows the feelings of confidence and self-esteem to be accessed very effectively.

CHAPTER 12
WARM-DOWN ACTIVITIES.

These are simple activities that reinforce a child's self-esteem. They are intended to help the filters to stay focused on positive aspects of the child and the world the child lives in. The reason we term them 'warm-down activities' is that the hard work has already been done with the other exercises described earlier in the training programme. These activities simply help a child's mind stay mentally 'supple' for the long-term future.

Affirmations.
An affirmation is a positive sentence that describes the way a person wants to be. They are usually short sentences that describe a specific quality that the individual wants to acquire. They are stated in the positive i.e. what the person wants, rather than what they *don't* want. Although they describe the way the individual wants to be, they are actually written in the present tense as if the individual already has the quality. Ideally, the affirmation should use words that are meaningful to the individual and they should describe actions and emotions. For example "I am always confident in all situations."

As we mentioned in Chapter 8, happiness is a habit that practice makes permanent, and affirmations are a relatively easy way to practice. A straightforward way to help a child to build this positive thinking activity into their daily routine is to help them to write four affirmations and then ask them to read the affirmations twice a day. It will help to reinforce the positive thoughts if, whilst reading the affirmations, the child imagines what they would see, hear and feel when they have achieved their affirmations. Utilising the modalities which we mentioned earlier when discussing NLP, engages a variety of the child's senses which increases the potency of this exercise.

Placing the written affirmations where they are visible is also a useful ploy. Attaching them to a mirror, a picture, the fridge or anywhere the child is likely to see them will remind them to repeat the affirmations regularly. Some children photocopy the affirmations and have them in more than one location.

Goal Setting.

Planning enjoyable activities well ahead appears to work well with children, and we described some similar exercises in the chapter on jogging. Goal setting differs from the previous exercises because by planning ahead children create positive DVDs about what the future *could* look like. It raises children's expectations of themselves and encourages them to think of different possibilities. This has a beneficial effect in countering the negative thoughts, and a bright picture of the future can help motivate children when they are trying to cope with difficult times in the present.

It's important that a child has had some experience of doing the previous exercises in the mental fitness programme before they embark on goal setting. Children who are locked into a negative thinking pattern of self-doubt, lack of confidence, low self-esteem and negative self-fulfilling prophecy are unlikely to be able to make much progress with setting themselves goals for the future.

Goal setting has the advantage of giving children clarity about what they want to achieve in the longer term and helps them formulate a series of steps to help them get there.

There are a number of steps to setting goals and the following guide can be used to help children through each step:

Step 1 – Make an inventory of your dreams.

This is a lovely phrase, which the author Anthony Robbins uses in his work on motivation (1). Ask the child to spend about fifteen minutes writing a brainstorm of everything they would like to have, do and be in two years' time. Encourage them not to limit themselves, allow them to let their minds roam free, the object of step 1 is simply to generate as many exciting possibilities as they can. They should aim to cover all the aspects of their lives - school, home, hobbies, friends, clubs, sports, jobs, pets – at this stage the more the better.

Step 2 – Define your ideal world in 12 months.
The next stage is to look at all the ideas that the brainstorm has generated and select about three to five goals that appear both desirable and achievable. It is important to get children to stretch themselves but at the same time the goals should be based on ability not bravado. For example a 14 year old lad might have written that in two years' time he wants to a be a professional football player. If he's been blessed with a tremendous amount of ability this may be possible and worthy of inclusion as a goal. However if he's only got a moderate amount of ability a better goal might be to become a sports coach which may still be desirable but is certainly more achievable. Again encourage the child to try to cover as many aspects of their lives as possible.

Step 3 – Define each goal precisely.
Invite the child to take the handful of goals that they've selected and define what they will see, hear and feel when they have successfully achieved each goal.

Step 4 – Challenge.
Without being over ambitious in terms of the amount of time available to achieve each goal in the next two years, encourage the child to challenge themselves to make the goal that little bit bigger or bolder.

Step 5 – Goal Setting Template.
By using a simple goal setting template children can write down their goals for the next two years and then break these down into milestones for twelve months, nine months, six months and three months. They can utilise some of the work from other training activities in helping to create their vision of the future.

Step 6 - Review the goals weekly.
Whether the child keeps the goals electronically or in a note book they should be encouraged to review them each week and write down anything they have done that week which is contributing towards achieving the goals. They should record all the activities even those that have been less successful because this still reinforces the fact that they have been active in trying to achieve their goals.

Some simple examples of goal setting are included on the following pages.

Two year goal setting template: Sports Coach.

Two year dream: To be employed as sports coach during the summer holidays.

Precise definition: I will see myself coaching a group of younger children who are all enjoying themselves. I can hear myself giving them clear instructions as I teach them various aspects of the sport. I will feel really confident and will be proud of what I've achieved.

12 month goal: To have gained at least one coaching qualification.
To have gained some experience as a volunteer coach.

9 month milestones: I will have successfully passed a coaching qualification.
I will be making enquiries about volunteering to assist adult coaches.

6 month milestones: I will have enrolled on a coaching course. I will be managing my time better to allow me to take the course.

3 month milestones: I will research what courses are available on the internet and at the local library. I will ask my PE teacher for his advice. I will have found out the cost of courses and make sure I can get the funding for the course and the necessary equipment. I will have got a job delivering newspapers to help earn the money to fund the above.

Two year goal setting template: Keyboard Player.

Two year dream: I want to be able to play keyboards confidently enough to be performing well in public e.g. in a local youth band or orchestra.

Precise definition: I will see myself playing in front of an audience. I can hear myself playing a particular piece of music and it is perfect. I will feel really confident and will be proud of what I've achieved.

12 month goal: To have performed at school assembly or in the school production. To successfully pass the keyboards grade exam.

9 month milestones: To ask my music teacher to allow me to
practice after school two days a week.
To persuade the drama teacher to let me
perform at the school production.

6 month milestones: To ask my music teacher to allow me to
practice at lunchtimes.
To perform at family gatherings when the
opportunity arises.

3 month milestones: I will get some help from my Aunt Jane who
plays the piano.
I will ask for some useful books and CDs on
playing keyboards for my birthday.

These are just simple examples. The goals could refer to anything
that the child has a desire and an ability to achieve.

As we mentioned before, the goals should be built on ability not
bravado, so a better understanding of the child's uniqueness clearly
helps. Children may also be able to use the previous exercises on
decision making and increasing their circle of influence to help
make their goals more achievable.

Warm-down activities are really the icing on the cake. They help
to keep children's confidence and self-esteem in good shape for the
future. By the time you've got to this stage of the mental fitness
programme the child should already have a healthy and balanced
perspective on life.

Summary of Chapter 12
Warm-down activities.

Affirmations.
An affirmation is a positive sentence that describes how a person wants to be. Affirmations are usually short sentences describing specific qualities and are stated in the positive. Although they describe the way the individual wants to be, they are written in the present tense as if the individual already has the quality.

It will help to reinforce the positive thoughts if, whilst reading the affirmations, the child imagines what they would see, hear and feel when they have achieved their affirmations. Utilising these modalities, which we mentioned earlier when discussing NLP, engages a variety of the child's senses which increases the potency of this exercise.

Goal Setting.
Goal setting is about formally planning to achieve something in the future. It creates positive DVDs about what the future *could* look like. It raises children's expectations of themselves and encourages them to think of different possibilities, which has a beneficial effect in countering negative thoughts. A bright picture of the future can also help motivate children when they are trying to cope with difficult times in the present.

It's important that a child has had some experience of doing the previous exercises in the mental fitness programme before they embark on goal setting. Children who are locked into a negative thinking pattern are unlikely to be able to make much progress with setting themselves goals for the future. The goals should be built on ability not bravado so a better understanding of a child's uniqueness clearly helps. They may also be able to use the previous exercises on decision making and increasing their sphere of influence, which can help make their goals more achievable.

SUMMARY
THE PROMISED LAND FOR CHILDREN.

Hopefully, through the concepts in this book, we've been able to lead you along the way to finding the Promised Land for Children. Our journey started out by explaining that psychological distress seems to be much more prevalent in the 21st century. There are a whole raft of sociological changes, which seem to have implications for our mental health generally, and the psychological well being of children in particular. Changes in family life such as increasing divorce rates, smaller families with less sibling support and less support from the extended family network have had a negative effect on children's psychological well-being.

The increasingly complex relationship we have with our work and the elusive work/life balance has also made an impact on our levels of psychological distress, which in turn affects our children. Rates of psychological illness have increased dramatically and the picture of child and adolescent health reflects this with spiralling rates of depression and suicide in this age group. However, the outlook need not be so gloomy. If we are able to help raise children's self-esteem it will give them the emotional resilience to combat psychological distress and to lead happy and fulfilled lives despite the pressures of the 21st century.

To take our first steps towards the Promised Land it is important to understand how our mind works when stress, anxiety and depression affect us. In order to do this we introduced a number of concepts. The first concept was the mind as a library full of DVDs, which represents the memory bank of our experiences of life. The increased prevalence of anxiety, stress and depression in a child's life is reflected by an increase in the number of negative DVDs in their library.

The next concept was the filter (the Reticular Activating System), which, when children are suffering from psychological distress, is set to notice the negative DVDs. The filter is kept firmly in place by thinking errors, which are a set of negative assumptions children make about themselves.

The last concept in this section of the book was the cycle of negative thinking. When children are constantly fed negative images of their lives and themselves it leads to self-doubt, which leads to lack of confidence and low self-esteem, which in turn can eventually lead to negative self-fulfilling prophecies. The section on threat sensitivity, risk aversion and the consequent tendency towards pessimism that can occur as a result, highlights this cycle of negative thinking.

We then spent some time looking at the way that children interact with their external world. The model we used for this was The Human Factors Model. We presented a theory that linked a child's values to their traits and styles – which all equate to their internal make-up. We then noted how the mismatch between a child's internal make-up and their external world (in the form of negative life events or situations) causes a negative impact on their mood state.

Our deliberations then turned to why some children may be more susceptible to stress, anxiety and depression than others. It seems that this is because of the tendency in some children towards threat sensitivity, which is often developed early in life. We also touched on the concept of fundamental attribution error and noted how people often attach too much blame to themselves (or others) without giving sufficient regard to the circumstances they find themselves in. Fundamental attribution error can have a further damaging effect on children's self-esteem.

The next milestone on our journey was the concept of control. The lesson we learned here is to accept that we can only control our own behaviour. If we help children to channel their energies into controlling what they can, and letting go of what they can't, they will feel more positive about themselves. Increasing their circle of influence helps achieve this. We also recognised the need to balance pessimism and blind optimism through the Stockdale paradox, when times are tough we must help children to face up to the brutal truth but remain optimistic that they will eventually overcome their difficulties.

We spent a little time exploring the idea of the mind's immune system and how it tries to quarantine very shocking and painful DVD memories by isolating them in a box. We talked about how important it is to help children to gently lift the lid on the box in order to dilute the power these particular negative memories may hold over them.

As we moved towards the latter stages of our journey we introduced our final concept – the mental fitness programme. The exercises in the programme are specifically designed to help children to practice positive thinking so that they can begin to eradicate the thinking errors. The warm-up activities start to gently stretch children's minds, jogging exercises begin to help them to look for positive experiences in the present and immediate future. Long steady runs teach them important lessons for life. The short sprints are techniques for combating more specific challenges, and the warm-down activities help stretch their positive thinking into the future.

Even for children, life is not for the fainthearted - into every life a little rain must fall. However, by understanding the concepts mentioned above and by practising positive thinking we can help to improve children's confidence and raise their self-esteem, which, as we said at the outset of the book, is probably the best gift you can ever give your children.

An appeal on behalf of less fortunate children.

Rick and Wendy each support a charity that helps children. Please consider making a donation to one (or both!) of the charities listed overleaf.

Many thanks.

Rick is donating 10% of his royalties to PAPYRUS, which is a national charity committed to the prevention of young suicide and the promotion of positive mental health and well being. It was founded in 1997 by a group of parents who had lost children to suicide and whose mission was to try to prevent this happening to other young people and their families.

PAPYRUS aims to raise awareness amongst the general public, professionals and policy makers of the need to address suicide prevention in society. It promotes examples of good practice in this area, and it provides practical help to anyone who may be concerned that someone they know may be at risk of taking their own lives.

PAPYRUS resources are used extensively in all areas of health and education. Thousands of leaflets and booklets are distributed each year, reaching those in need of help through other organisations, such as Child and Adolescent Mental Health teams, Connexions, A&E and Psychiatric Liaison staff.

The charity's helpline – **HOPElineUK** - **0870 170 4000** – is unique in that it is staffed by paid mental health professionals who can give support, information and practical advice on what to do if the caller is worried that someone they know may be thinking of taking their own life. The cost of running the helpline service currently exceeds £90,000 and costs are rising as the call rate increases.

As a small charity working in a much-neglected field the demands on PAPYRUS are increasing day by day. PAPYRUS's commitment and valuable contribution to suicide prevention in young people depends on the goodwill and generosity of its supporters.

Every donation received helps us to continue to play our part in preventing suicide.

"At the end of the day, when you're out of your mind with worry, where can you turn for help? PAPYRUS was there for me at a time when I needed it most."

131

For more information about PAPYRUS and its work, or to send a donation write to PAPYRUS, The Lodge, Thompson Park, Ormerod Road, BURNLEY BB11 2RU

Tel: 01282 432555 email: admin@papyrus-uk.org

www.papyrus-uk.org

Registered Charity No. 1070896

A Company Limited By Guarantee No: 3555482

Wendy has been working with Ethiopian Teachers in Addis Ababa to encourage and support the development of spoken English, which is an essential skill to allow for further development of the country. As a trustee of the charity she can see the value of working in the developing world.

If you feel able to support this work we have a covenant and gift aid method, for a form please email marioneng@waitrose.com or send cheques to the address below.

You can also support this work by collecting books and organising fund raising events. For more information go to http://www.cruwys.info/index.html

CRUWYS GLOBAL TRUST

Preparing 21st Century
Global Citizens

UK Contact

Mrs Marion Englefield
Jordans
Dunbridge Lane
Awbridge
Romsey, SO51 0GQ

Trustees:
Wendy Forrest-Charde
Rosemary Green
John Green
Marion Englefield

Cruwys Global Trust is a registered charity, the trust operates in the UK, and with local partners in Ethiopia and elsewhere.

The objects of the trust are

- The advancement of education within Ethiopia
- The promotion of quality English Language provision within Ethiopia
- The promotion of international understanding of development issues in the UK, Ethiopia and elsewhere

Cruwys Global Trust has been created in order to give opportunities for the less privileged to improve their lot in life through education. It also supports needy individuals in extremely practical ways. To date more than 20,000 books have been collected for use in Cruwys partner organisations. So far more than 300 needy people have benefited by sponsorships and scholarships. Educational resources have been donated to libraries, special needs schools, and other projects in the countryside as well as Addis Ababa.

When we work on professional development with our main partner institutions we ensure that local, less privileged schools are invited to send teachers and that those teachers leave with donations of appropriate resources.

LIST OF APPENDICES.

Appendix 1 – Positive Listing Exercise.

Appendix 2 – Thinking Errors.

Appendix 3 – Diary Keeping.

Appendix 4 – Well Formed Outcomes.

Appendix 5 – Affirmations.

Appendix 6 – Goal Setting.

APPENDIX 1 – POSITIVE LISTING EXERCISE.

Make a list of 20 positive things in your life. The list can include: things you are good at; activities you enjoy; friends and family who care about you; achievements you are proud of; things that make you laugh.

There are no right or wrong answers, the list can include anything from any time in your life. It might be easier to write down two or three things each day to gradually build up your list.

1._____

2._____

3._____

4._____

5._____

6._____

7._____

8._____

9._____

10._____

11._____

12._____

13._____

14._____

15._____

16._____

17._____

18._____

19._____

20._____

APPENDIX 2 – THINKING ERRORS

1. All or Nothing Thinking. Things are perceived in black or white categories. Anything short of perfection is viewed as a failure.

2. Over Generalisation. A single negative event is perceived as a never-ending pattern of defeat. The word "always" is often used to describe negative events and "never" to describe positive events.

3. Disqualifying the Positives. Positive experiences are described as not counting – it was easy, anyone can do that.

4. Jumping to Conclusions. Negative interpretations occur even though there are no facts to support the conclusion e.g. "everyone's got it in for me today."

5. Magnification and Minimisation. Magnifying your own errors or other people's achievements. Minimising your own achievements or other people's errors.

6. Emotional Reason. Assuming that your negative emotions reflect the way things really are.

7. Should Statements. When directed inwards, at oneself, they encourage failure or defeat. When directed at others they encourage anger, frustration and resentment.

8. Labelling and mislabelling. An extreme form of generalisation. Instead of describing an error you attach a negative label to yourself or others e.g. "I'm hopeless." "She is an idiot." "It was the worst day of my life." The language is often highly coloured or emotionally loaded.

9. Personalisation. Seeing yourself or someone else as the cause of some negative external event which, in fact, you or the other person, were not responsible for.

APPENDIX 3 – DIARY KEEPING.

At the end of every day write down a few sentences to describe what happened over the course of the day. Then rate your day in terms of how it felt:

1 = It was a terrible day to 10 = It was a fantastic day.

If the score for the day is on the low side, read the list of thinking errors to see if you are making any negative assumptions about your day which, if successfully challenged, will prove to be false. As a result of the successful challenges your scores may improve.

Recording your thoughts and feelings on the day that they occur is a powerful way of helping you to do a number of things:

➤ It allows you to make comparisons between days.

➤ You can track patterns to see whether there are certain triggers that cause you to score certain days higher or lower than others.

➤ Most importantly, it gives you a chance to challenge your thinking errors as they occur.

APPENDIX 4 – WELL FORMED OUTCOMES.

1. "What outcomes do you want to achieve from this?"

This is a very broad question but try to be clear about what you want to achieve. There are no right or wrong answers to this question, just write down what you feel you want to achieve. It's worth remembering that if you want to be able to measure your progress towards the outcome, the more specific your answer is then the easier it is to see how much progress you're making towards the outcome.

2. "Where, when and with who do you want to achieve your outcomes?"

This helps to make things clearer. Sometimes we have a specific problem related to home life or school for example or it may be a confidence problem dealing with a specific group of people. Putting a realistic time frame on achieving the outcomes can also help chart your progress.

3. "What will it look, sound and feel like when I've achieved my outcomes?"

Using your imagination can be very important in helping to motivate you when the effort seems too much. Having an attractive picture of what the future holds encourages us to achieve our outcomes.

4. "Are you in control of the changes necessary to help you achieve your outcomes?"

Try to think about what you can and can't control, what you need to accept Vs what you need to change, and where you should channel your energies.

5. "Will I lose anything if I succeed in achieving my outcomes?"

Sometimes we end up losing things if we succeed in achieving our outcomes, but the loss may be worth it because of the potential gains. Taking a stand against something we feel is wrong might mean we could lose a group of friends.

6. "Is the outcome worth the effort?"

If you don't think the outcome is worth the effort you need to ask some more questions. Are you really clear about the benefits of making your thinking more positive? Do you understand the negative long-term effects of not changing your thinking? If, on the other hand, the outcome *is* worth the effort then don't cheat on how much honest effort you put into trying to change your thinking.

7. "What will all the positive consequences be of achieving my outcomes?"

List as many benefits that will come from being able to re-set your filter to notice all the positive things in your life. This answer may be similar to some of your previous answers but that's a good thing – it reaffirms what you already know - that the outcome will be worth the effort.

APPENDIX 5 – AFFIRMATIONS.

Affirmations are usually short sentences that describe a specific quality that you want to acquire. They are stated in the positive i.e. what you want, rather than what you *don't* want. Although they describe the way you want to be, they are actually written in the present tense as if you already have the quality. Ideally the affirmation should use words that are meaningful to you and they should describe actions and emotions. For example "I am always confident in all situations."

Write down four affirmations and read the affirmations twice a day.

Affirmation 1.

Affirmation 2.

Affirmation 3.

Affirmation 4.

Whilst reading the affirmations imagine what you would see, hear and feel when you have achieved your affirmations.

Put the written affirmations where you can see them. Attaching them to a mirror, a picture, the fridge or anywhere you are likely to see them will remind you to repeat the affirmations regularly. Some children photocopy the affirmations and have them in more than one location.

APPENDIX 6 – GOAL SETTING.

Step 1 – Make an inventory of your dreams. Spend about fifteen minutes brainstorming everything you would like to have, do and be in two years time. Don't limit yourself, allow your mind to roam free, generate as many exciting possibilities as you can. Try to cover all the aspects of your life - school, home, hobbies, friends, clubs, sports, jobs, pets or anything else that is important to you.

Step 2 – Define your ideal world in 12 months. From the brainstorm select about three to five goals that appear both desirable and achievable. Stretch yourself but at the same time the goals should be based on your ability. For example a 14 year old lad might write down that in two years time he wants to a be a professional footballer. If he's got a tremendous amount of ability this may be possible and worthy of inclusion as a goal. However if he's only got a moderate amount of ability a better goal might be to become a sports coach which may still be desirable but is certainly more achievable.

Step 3 – Define each goal precisely. Take the handful of goals that you've selected and define what you will see, hear and feel when you have successfully achieved each goal.

Step 4 – Challenge. Without being over ambitious in terms of the amount of time available to achieve each goal in the next 12 months, challenge yourself to make the goal that little bit bigger or bolder.

Step 5 – Goal Setting Template. By using the simple goal setting template write down your goals for the next 12 months and then break these down into milestones for 9 months, 6 months and three months.

Step 6 - Review the goals weekly. Review the goals each week and write down anything you've done that week which is contributing to your progress towards the goals.

An example of goal setting:

Two year dream: To be employed as sports coach during the summer holidays.

Precise definition: I will see myself coaching a group of younger children who are all enjoying themselves. I can hear myself giving them clear instructions as I teach them various aspects of the sport. I will feel really confident and will be proud of what I've achieved.

12 month goal: To have gained at least one coaching qualification.
To have gained some experience as a volunteer coach.

9 month milestones: I will have successfully passed a coaching qualification.
I will be making enquiries about volunteering to assist adult coaches.

6 month milestones: I will have enrolled on a coaching course.
I will be managing my time better to allow me to take the course.

3 month milestones: I will research what courses are available on the internet and at the local library.
I will ask my PE teacher for his advice.
I will have found out the cost of courses and make sure I can get the funding for the course and the necessary equipment.
I will have got a job delivering newspapers to help earn the money to fund the above.

Template.

Two year dream:

Precise definition:

12 month goal:

9 month milestones:

6 month milestones:

3 month milestones:

Notes.

Notes.

Notes.

Notes.

Notes.

Notes.

Notes.

Notes.

REFERENCES.

Introduction.
1. Norris, R. W. (2005) *The Promised Land – a guide to positive thinking for sufferers of stress, anxiety and depression.* Authorhouse.
2. The Mental Health Foundation. (1999). *Bright Futures – promoting Children and Young People's Mental Health* [online]. Available from World Wide Webb: http://www.mhf.org.uk

Chapter 1.
1. UK Office for National Statistics. (2005) [online].
2. Summerfield, C., and Babb, P (2004). *Social Trends* [online]. Available from World Wide Web: http://www.statistics .gov.uk
3. Schwartz, J. (2004) Workplace Stress: Americans' Bugaboo. *New York Times,* **05 September 2004,** p.D2.
4. Barham, C. and Begum, N. (2006) *Labour Market Trends* [online] **113**(4), pp149 –158 National Statistics. Available from World Wide Web: http://www.statistics .gov.uk
5. Anon. (2006) *A Guide to Women Returners and Employers* [online]. Available from World Wide Web: http://www.dti.gov.ukfiles
6. Tomlinson, J., Olsen, W., Fagen, D. & Purdam, K. (2005) *Maximising the potential of women returners in areas of high occupational segregation.* University of Manchester.
7. Gregg, P. & Waldfogel, J. (2005) Symposium of parental leave. Early maternal employment and child outcomes. *The Economic Journal,* **115** (F1-F6).
8. Deeks, E. (2000) *People Management..*
9. Chartered Institute of Personnel and Development website (2005) [online].
10. Confederation of British Industry Statistics. (2004).
11. World Health Organisation Report, 11.04.01 [online].
12. World Health Organisation Report, 4.10.01 [online].

Chapter 2.
1. Office for National Statistics [online] ONS website document 8986.xls. Available from World Wide Web: http://www. papyrus.org.uk.
2. Moscicki, E. K.(2001) Epidemiology of completed and attempted suicide: toward a framework for prevention. *Clinical Neuroscience Research*, **1,** pp310-23.
3. Murakami, S., Otsuka, K., Kubo,Y., Shinagawa, M., Yamanaka, T., Ohkawa, S. & Kitaura, Y. (2004) Repeated ambulatory monitoring reveals a Monday morning surge in blood pressure in a community-dwelling population. *American Journal of Hypertension,* **17**(12,) pp1179-1183.
4. *Psychology Today* (1999). **March 1999.**
5. *US National Institute of Health Publication* (1999) Number 00-4501
6. Coleman, J. & Schofield, J. (2005) *Key Data on Adolescence.* 5th Ed., Brighton: Trust for Study of Adolescence.
7. Norris, R. W. (2005) *The Promised Land – a guide to positive thinking for sufferers of stress, anxiety and depression.* Authorhouse.

Chapter 3.
1. Kensinger, E. A. & Schacter, D. L. (2006) When the Red Sox shocked the Yankees. Comparing negative and positive memories. *Psychonomic Bulletin and Review,* **13**, pp757-763.
2. Rath, T. and Clifton, D. (2004) *How full is your bucket?* Gallup Press.
3. Seligman, M.E.P. and Schulman, P. (1986) Explanatory style as a predictor of productivity and quitting among life insurance agents. *Journal of Personality and Social Psychology,* **50**, pp832 – 838.
4. Burns, D. (1980) *Feeling Good. The new mood therapy.* Avon Paperbacks.

Chapter 4.
1. Bengston, V. L., Bilbarz, T. J. & Roberts, R. (2002) *How Families Still Matter - A Longitudinal Study of Youth in Two Generations.* Cambridge: University Press

2. Psychometrics Ltd. (1997) *The Jung Type Inventory.* Psytech International Ltd.
3. Buckingham, M. and Clifton, D. (2002) *Now discover your strengths.* Simon and Schuster.
4. Robbins, A. (1986) *Unlimited Power.* Simon and Schuster Ltd.
5. Kolb, D. A. (1993) *Learning Style Inventory.* Boston: Hay/ McBer.

Chapter 5.
1. Jones, E. E. and Harris, V. A. (1967). The attribution of attitudes. *Journal of Experimental Social Psychology* **3**, pp1 – 24.
2. Nisbett, R. E. and Ross, L. (1991) *The Person and the Situation.* Philadelphia: Temple University Press.
3. Grehardt, S. (2004) *Why Love Matters.* Routledge.
4. Westen, D. & Harnden-Fischer, J. (2001) Personality profiles in eating disorders. *American Journal of Psychiatry,* **158**(4), pp547-62.
5. Marmot, M. (1994) Work and other factors influencing coronary health and sickness absence. *Work and Stress*, **8,** pp191 – 201.
6. Glasser, W. (1998) *Choice Theory.* Harper Perennial.
7. Collins, J. (2001) *Good to great: Why some companies make the leap and others don't.* Harper Business.

Chapter 7.
1. Maltz, M. (1960). *Psycho-cybernetics.* Prentice Hall.

Chapter 9.
1. Russell, G. F. (2005) *Big Rocks.* Sausalito, CA: Lifestyle Press.

Chapter 10.
1. Fairweather, A. K., Anstey, K. J., Rodgers, B. & Butterworth, P. (2006) Factors distinguishing suicide attempters from suicide ideators in a community sample: social issues and physical health problems. *Psychological Medicine,* **36**, pp1235-1245.

Chapter 11.
1. Bandler, R. and Grinder, J. (1975) *The structure of magic.* Science in Behaviour Books.
2. Fairweather, A. K., Anstey, K. J., Rodgers, B. & Butterworth, P. (2006) Factors distinguishing suicide attempters from suicide ideators in a community sample: social issues and physical health problems. *Psychological Medicine,* **36**, pp1235-1245.
3. Covey, S. R. (1989) *The seven habits of highly effective people.* Simon and Schuster UK.
4. Robbins, A. (1986) *Unlimited power.* Simon and Schuster Ltd.

Chapter 12.
1. Robbins, A. (1986) *Unlimited power.* Simon and Schuster Ltd.

3842102R00101

Printed in Great Britain
by Amazon.co.uk, Ltd.,
Marston Gate.